Wok

Edited by Fred Sandman

D1416168

BARNES & NOBLE

NEW YORK

contents

Infinite Variety
The Basic Ingredients

With the rising popularity of the Asian cuisine, the wok has become increasingly popular in the West, too. As in any Asian kitchen, you can use it to fry, braise and deep-fry to your heart's content. Far-Eastern meals fascinate us owing to their variety and bewitching flavors. Ample herbs and spices, a lot of fresh vegetables, little meat, lean fish and a sheer endless choice of exquisitely aromatic pastes and sauces are used lavishly. The fine ingredients are cooked for only a very short time in the wok, leaving both the taste and vitamins intact. It's worth taking a trip to the world of an Asian food store. While initially some things will be confusing at first, these strange items will wander into your shopping basket on your next visit. And if there's no Asian store in your neighborhood, do not worry: Many of these ingredients are already available in most good supermarkets. Really exotic ingredients can be ordered on the internet. But success is only guaranteed if the ingredients are fresh. If you have ever cooked with fresh ginger or lemongrass, you will never use the dried or powdered varieties again. Don't forget that a wok is not just for Asian cooking. Whatever can be fried in the pan can be prepared just as well in the wok. So, let's get to wok!

SCALLIONS (left), sometimes also known as spring or green onions, have a mild flavor. However, it is not only the pale section, but also the herby green that is used in wok cooking. For garnishing, cut the green into long strips, then drop into icy water and it will curl up into a beautiful flower shape.

1 **CHILI PEPPERS**, the fiery hot relatives of bell peppers, add pungency to wok dishes. Unripe chilies are green, ripe ones red. In general, small chilies are hotter than large ones.

2 **LEMONGRASS** is a reed-like plant. It has a lemony fragrance and flavor, but also a mild heat. Only the tender lower part of the stalks is used.

3 **RICE VINEGAR** is significantly milder than ordinary vinegar as it has an acidity of just three per cent.

4 **SHIITAKE MUSHROOMS**, also called Tongu mushrooms, have a very strong aroma. They are available all year round.

5 **BASMATI** is the most exquisite of long-grain varieties of rice, with a fine flavor and typical aroma. It is also known as aromatic rice and is ideal for frying.

6 **CILANTRO,** the green leaves of the coriander plant, is used in many different ways in Asian cooking: Cilantro green is used like parsley. The seeds have a flowery sweet flavor.

7 **TOFU** is made from curdled soy bean milk. It can be cut and is rich in protein, but low in cholesterol. When fresh, it is very mild, when smoked, it is slightly spicy.

BAMBOO SHOOTS are the young shoots of the bamboo plant. They are harvested like asparagus by cutting when they reach a height of 1 foot. They are available in cans.

HOISIN SAUCE is used in China to season meat and poultry dishes. The thick, dark sauce is made of soy beans, water, vinegar, sugar, garlic, chili and sesame seeds.

GINGER seasons from spicy fruity to burning hot, depending on the amount used. Use only the root of the plant, which, when freshly ground, produces a unique aroma.

LIME LEAVES come from the kaffir lime tree. They are dark green, leathery firm and smell very much of limes.

NOODLES in Asia are made of wheat, buckwheat or whole-grain flour. Rice noodles (made from rice flour) are a specialty, as are the transparent glass noodles made from mung bean starch.

SESAME OIL is pressed from roasted sesame seeds. It has a strong nutty flavor and brown color.

SOY SAUCE is considered the universal seasoning in the Asian kitchen. The dark salty sauces from China and Japan are very popular. The light, milder varieties are used for fish and vegetable dishes since they do not color the ingredients.

WONTON (or wan-tan) wrappers come from China. The light yellow sheets are made from all-purpose wheat flour and eggs. You can buy them fresh or frozen.

Step by Step
Cooking in Asia

Food lovers and professional cooks both swear equally by the incredibly versatile genius of Asian cuisine: Whether boiling, frying, steaming, braising, stir-frying or deep-frying – there is hardly anything you cannot do with a wok. Traditional woks are made of hammered iron or steel, with a rounded base and sloping sides. The modern variety is made of cast aluminum which allows for the heat to be distributed more evenly. Generally, gas stoves are better suited for woks than electric stoves. The heat is immediate and can be regulated more precisely. For electric stoves, cast iron woks, stainless steel woks or those made of carbon steel are best suited. The most important utensils (spatula, chopsticks for stirring, a draining rack and a wooden frame for the steaming insert) are usually supplied with the wok when bought new. The wok should come with a lid for steaming and braising purposes. The most important rule for cooking in a wok: All the ingredients have to be prepared very carefully and cut into very small pieces. Cooking itself is very quick and uncomplicated.

Steaming – Step by step to success

1 Put the clean wok onto the stove and place a wooden rack inside for the bamboo basket.

4 Fill the wok one-third with water. Cover and bring the water to a boil.

2 Alternately, you can place a small plate or even a small bowl upside down in the wok.

5 Arrange the food to be cooked in the bamboo basket, cover and cook in the wok until done.

3 Then position the bamboo basket on the wooden frame.

6 If you do not have a bamboo basket, use a small plate instead and put it on the wooden rack for steaming.

Stir-frying – made easy

1 Heat the wok, add the oil and distribute evenly in the wok. First sear the garlic and the onions in the oil.

2 Then add the prepared ingredients to the oil: first the vegetable and meat pieces with the longest cooking times.

3 Stir the ingredients constantly. The strong heat ensures that the flavor, color and nutritive value remain intact. Move anything cooked to the edge of the wok.

4 Mix the ingredients for the sauce in a small bowl, add to the wok, a spoonful at a time, and mix in carefully.

Preparing chili peppers

1 Cut the chili peppers in half lengthwise. Remove the stems, seeds and white inner walls. Rinse the peppers and pat dry.

2 Cut the chili peppers in rings. Be careful: Chili peppers are very hot, so always wash your hands after cutting them.

Preparing wontons

1 Arrange the sheets of wonton pastry beside one another and allow to defrost. Brush the left and upper edges with beaten egg white.

2 Place some prepared filling (made of vegetables, meat or shrimp) on the lower half of each sheet, a spoonful at a time, as shown on the picture.

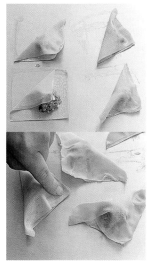

3 Fold the left upper corner diagonally over the lower right corner. Or bring all four corners up and twist together to make a pouch.

4 Press the edges of the triangles together well with your fingers. Wontons can be steamed, deep-fried or used in soups.

Vegetarian

Steamed Wontons
Filled with Spinach

Authenically Asian: These little snacks with their spicy
fillings are quick to make and always good for a surprise

Ingredients

½ pound leaf spinach
(frozen)
20 wonton wrappers (frozen)
4 mushrooms · 2 scallions
2 ounces bamboo shoots
(canned)
1 teaspoon freshly grated
ginger · 1 garlic clove
1 teaspoon cornstarch
2 teaspoons sesame oil
sugar
salt · freshly ground pepper
some lettuce leaves

Preparation

SERVES 4

1 Allow the spinach to defrost, squeeze out well and chop finely. Lay the wonton wrappers out individually, cover with a damp dishtowel and allow to defrost for about 30 minutes.

2 Prepare, wash and finely chop the mushrooms and scallions. Allow the bamboo shoots to drain in a sieve and dice finely.

3 Mix the mushrooms, scallions and bamboo shoots with the grated ginger. Peel the garlic, chop finely and add to the vegetables. Stir in the cornstarch and 1 teaspoon sesame oil, season with a pinch of sugar, salt and pepper.

4 Place one teaspoon of filling into the center of each wrapper. Bring the edges of the pastry up over the filling and press together lightly – there should be a little filling visible in the middle.

5 Bring two cups water to a boil ensuring that the bottom of the steamer does not touch the water. Line the steamer or bamboo basket with the washed lettuce leaves. Arrange the wontons on the lettuce, cover and steam for about 10 minutes in the wok. Sprinkle the remaining sesame oil over and serve immediately.

Tip

Wonton wrappers, which are made of wheat and egg pastry, are available frozen in Asian food stores. Just take the required number from the package and save the rest for another time.

Deep-fried Wontons
with Coconut and Vegetables

A big occasion for little specialties: Crisp packets of pastry with a spicy filling are all the rage as finger food

Ingredients

20 sheets wonton pastry
(frozen)

2 scallions

1 carrot

5 1/2 ounces sweet corn
(canned)

2 1/2 ounces fresh coconut

5 tablespoons soy sauce

freshly ground pepper

vegetable oil, for frying

Preparation

SERVES 4

1 Lay the wonton sheets out individually, cover with a damp dishtowel and allow to defrost for about 30 minutes.

2 Meanwhile prepare the scallions, wash and cut into very fine rings. Peel the carrot and grate coarsely. Pour the corn into a sieve, rinse briefly and allow to drain.

3 For the filling, grate the coconut very finely into a bowl. Add the scallions, carrot and corn, season to taste with soy sauce and pepper and mix well.

4 Place 1 heaped teaspoon of the filling in the center of each wonton sheet. Brush the edges of the pastry with water, lift and carefully twist together above the filling to make a pouch.

5 Heat the oil in the wok over high heat. Deep-fry the wontons in the oil until golden brown. Remove with a slotted spoon and allow to drain on paper towels.

Tip

Why not try wontons with a filling made of 10 1/2 ounces peeled, seeded and chopped tomatoes, 4 1/2 ounces chopped Mozzarella, seasoned with garlic, basil, parsley, salt and pepper.

Spring Rolls
with Chinese Vegetables

Ingredients

³/₄ ounce glass noodles

10 dried tree ear mushrooms

14 sheets spring roll pastry
(frozen)

6 ounces Chinese cabbage

1 piece fresh ginger root (size of
a hazelnut)

1 carrot (cut into fine strips)

1 bunch scallions (cut into thin
rings)

1 bunch chives (cut into rolls)

1-2 teaspoons sesame oil

salt · 1 tablespoon cornstarch

vegetable oil, for frying

Preparation
SERVES 4

1 Cover the glass noodles and mushrooms each
in a bowl with boiling water and allow to swell
for about 15 minutes. Lay out the sheets of
spring roll pastry and allow to defrost.

2 Prepare the Chinese cabbage, wash and shred
finely. Peel and chop the ginger. Allow the
noodles to drain and cut into ¹/₂-inch lengths
with scissors. Allow the mushrooms to drain
and cut into strips, removing the hard stems.
Mix the Chinese cabbage, carrot, scallions and
garlic with the noodles, mushrooms and ginger

and season with sesame oil and salt. Cut the
sheets of spring roll pastry in half. Mix the
cornstarch with about 1 tablespoons water.

3 Spoon a little vegetable filling onto the lower
half of the pastry sheets. Fold the edges over
the filling, brush with cornstarch and roll the
pastry up. Press the edges together well.

4 Heat the oil in the wok, deep-fry the spring
rolls, a few at a time, for 2-3 minutes until
golden brown. Allow to drain on paper towels
and keep warm in the oven until serving.

Dim Sum
with Onions and Bean Sprouts

Ingredients

2 scallions

1/2 yellow bell pepper

1 red chili pepper

1 garlic clove

1/3 cup bean sprouts

2 tablespoons sesame oil

1/3 cup soy sauce

2 cups wheat starch

1 tablespoon pickled ginger

Preparation
SERVES 4

1 Trim and wash the scallions and yellow bell pepper. Dice finely. Wash the chili, seed and chop very finely. Peel the garlic and also chop finely. Rinse the bean sprouts under hot water in a sieve, drain and chop coarsely.

2 Heat the oil in the preheated wok. Add the scallions, diced bell pepper, chili pepper, garlic and bean sprouts and cook for 2 minutes. Season with 1 tablespoon of the soy sauce and leave to cool.

3 Put the starch into a bowl, add a little boiling water gradually, stir and then knead until the dough is smooth.

4 Form 12 balls and roll them out into 4-inch circles. Place 1 tablespoon filling on the center of each pastry circle (or store-bought wrapper). Fold the pastry over the filling, press the edges together firmly and slightly crimp the sealed edge. Steam for 10 minutes in the wok in a bamboo basket or other steamer. Mix the ginger and the remaining soy sauce together and serve as a dip with the dim sum.

Spinach Parcels
with Curry Coconut Sauce

These parcels are an absolute delight: One of the best aspects
of steaming food is that a bit of culinary artistry can be applied

Ingredients

4 lime leaves

14 ounces large spinach
leaves

salt · 1 zucchini · 2 carrots

2 stalks green or white
asparagus

1 bunch scallions

1 fennel bulb

freshly ground pepper

a few stems chives (or kitchen
string)

2 garlic cloves

1 bunch basil

1 tablespoon lemon juice

2 teaspoons red curry paste

2 tablespoons unsweetened
coconut milk

Preparation

SERVES 4

1 Wash the lime leaves and cut into thin strips. Remove the stems from the spinach leaves. Wash the spinach leaves and blanch briefly in boiling salted water, allow to drain, and spread over the working surface.

2 Prepare and wash the vegetables. Cut the zucchini and carrots into sticks, the asparagus and scallions into 2-inch pieces. Cut the fennel crosswise into strips. Arrange the vegetables and strips of lime on the spinach leaves, salt and pepper. Roll up the spinach leaves and tie together with the chives or kitchen string.

3 Peel the garlic and chop finely. Wash the basil, pluck the leaves from the stems. Add the basil stems to the wok with the garlic. Add 1 cup water and the lemon juice, bring all to a boil. Place the vegetable parcels in the steamer, cover and cook for about 15 minutes in the wok until tender but still firm to the bite.

4 At the end of the cooking time, remove the steamer and keep the spinach parcels warm. Remove the basil stems from the stock. Bring the stock to a boil with curry paste and coconut milk and season to taste with salt. Add the basil leaves and cook briefly. Serve the sauce with the spinach parcels.

Tip

Vary the filling in the parcels as preferred. Why not add radish, garlic chives, or bok choy leaves to the spinach parcels?

Vegetable Tempura
with Papaya Dip

Ingredients

2 pounds green asparagus

7 ounces shiitake mushrooms

1 red bell pepper

1 red chili pepper

1 ½ ounces scallions

6 stalks garlic chives

1 papaya (about 14 ounces)

3-4 tablespoons light soy sauce

3-4 tablespoons lime juice

sugar

1 cup all-purpose flour

1 level teaspoon baking powder

1 egg

1 tablespoon dark soy sauce

peanut oil, for frying

Preparation

SERVES 4

1 Fill ¾ cup water into a plastic container and leave in the freezer for 20 minutes. Peel the lower third of the asparagus, wash and cut the stems into 3-inch pieces. Prepare the shiitake mushrooms. Prepare the bell peppers, wash and cut into strips.

2 Cut the chili peppers in half lengthwise, seed, wash and chop. Prepare the scallions, wash and cut into thin rings. Wash the garlic chives, shake dry and chop.

3 For the dip, cut the papaya in half lengthwise, seed and peel. Dice the flesh finely, mix with the light soy sauce and lime juice. Mix the chili, scallions, garlic cloves and 1 pinch sugar.

4 Mix the flour with the baking powder in a bowl. Whisk the egg, the iced water and the dark soy sauce. Stir in the flour mixture. The batter should be thin. Fill the oil into the wok until about ¾-inch high and heat. Toss the vegetables in the batter and fry for about 5 minutes in the oil until golden brown. Allow to drain on paper towels and serve with the dip.

Tofu Bites
with Lime Butter

Ingredients

2 limes

3 tablespoons light soy sauce

1 level teaspoon ground pepper

1 level teaspoon sugar

14 ounces tofu

1 stick butter

4 tablespoons vegetable oil

Preparation
SERVES 4

1 Wash the limes and rub dry. Finely grate the peel of 1 lime. Halve both limes and squeeze out the juice.

2 Make a marinade with the soy sauce, pepper, sugar and three quarters of the lime juice, stirring constantly until the sugar is completely dissolved.

3 Cut the tofu into slices 3/4-inch thick and brush both sides with the marinade. Allow the tofu slices to marinate for 15 minutes.

4 Beat the butter until fluffy. Stir in the grated lime peel and the remaining lime juice, a spoonful at a time.

5 Heat the wok over high heat and pour in the oil. Fry the tofu slices until golden brown on both sides.

6 Allow the lime butter to melt on the fried tofu slices. Remove the tofu bites from the wok and serve on a hot plate. Sprinkle with coarsely ground pepper (optional).

Asian Vegetables
with Tofu Slices

Something's stirring in the wok: When aromatic vegetables are
served with fried tofu, connoisseurs will be crying out for more

Ingredients

3 1/2 ounces each shiitake

mushrooms, oyster

mushrooms and portobello

mushrooms

1 red and 1 yellow bell pepper

10 ounces Chinese cabbage

7 ounces Chinese water

chestnuts (canned)

6 ounces tofu · 1 garlic clove

1/2 teaspoon red curry paste

1 tablespoon rice vinegar

2-3 tablespoons light soy

sauce · salt

2 tablespoons sesame oil

peanut oil, for frying

1 teaspoon cornstarch

1/3 cup vegetable stock

5 tablespoons cornflour

Preparation

SERVES 4

1 Prepare the mushrooms. Chop the stems of the shiitake mushrooms and cut the caps in half. Cut the oyster mushrooms into thin strips, halve the portobello mushrooms. Wash the bell peppers and Chinese cabbage. Cut the peppers into fine strips. Shred the cabbage coarsely. Allow the water chestnuts to drain in a sieve and cut in half. Rinse the tofu, dry on paper towels and cut into 1/4-inch slices. Peel and chop the garlic.

2 Stir the curry paste with 3 tablespoons hot water until smooth. Add the rice vinegar, soy sauce and salt. Sprinkle the marinade over the tofu and allow to stand for 15 minutes.

3 Heat the wok, add the sesame oil and 2 tablespoons peanut oil. Sear the mushrooms, stirring constantly. Add the Chinese cabbage, strips of bell peppers, water chestnuts and garlic. Stir-fry the vegetables for about 2 minutes.

4 Pour the tofu into a sieve, catch the marinade and reserve. Stir the cornflour into the marinade until smooth. Add the stock and the tofu marinade to the vegetables in the wok and allow to simmer briefly. Remove and keep warm.

5 Clean the wok using paper towels. Heat the peanut oil in the wok over high heat. Fill the cornflour into a deep plate and toss the tofu slices in it. Fry the tofu in the hot oil until golden brown, then allow to drain on paper towels. Serve the tofu slices on the vegetables.

Scrambled Eggs
with Chinese Mushrooms

A simple dish, but oh, so nice: Scrambled eggs are transformed in no time into an exotic spicy snack

Ingredients

3 dried morel mushrooms

3 dried shiitake mushrooms

1 small red chili pepper

1/4-inch piece fresh ginger root

2 scallions

2 sprigs cilantro

4 eggs

2 teaspoons light soy sauce

freshly ground black pepper

1 teaspoon peanut oil

1 teaspoon vegetable oil

Preparation

SERVES 4

1 Cover the dried mushrooms in a bowl with enough hot water to cover them completely. Allow them to swell for 15 minutes.

2 Cut the chili peppers in half lenghtwise, wash, seed and cut into fine strips. Peel the ginger and chop very finely. Trim the scallions, wash and cut into fine strips. Wash the cilantro, shake dry and pluck the leaves from the stems.

3 Drain the mushrooms, squeeze dry and cut into pieces. Beat the eggs and stir in the soy sauce, pepper to taste and the peanut oil.

4 Heat the vegetable oil in the preheated wok. Stir-fry the mushrooms briefly. Then add the rest of the ingredients, except for the eggs, and mix with the mushrooms. Pour in the beaten eggs and cook until they begin to set, pushing the mixture to the edge of the wok as it sets.

5 Serve the scrambled eggs on warmed plates or in small bowls, garnished with cilantro.

Tip

This scrambled egg dish can, of course, also be made with fresh mushrooms. Only wash the mushrooms if they are really dirty. Otherwise just rub them clean with paper towels.

Diced Tofu
with Vegetables

Ingredients

1 bunch young carrots

1 thick leek

2 kohlrabi

1 small broccoli

1 1/2 cups snow peas

salt

2 large tomatoes

6 tablespoons vegetable oil

freshly ground pepper

about 1/2 cup vegetable stock

14 ounces tofu

2 garlic cloves

1/2 bunch flat leaf parsley

Preparation

SERVES 4

1 Prepare and wash the vegetables, peel if necessary. Cut the carrots and leek into slices, and kohlrabi into sticks. Separate the broccoli into small flowerets. Blanch the flowerets and snow peas separately in boiling salted water, dip briefly into cold water and allow to drain. Cut an X into the top and bottom of the tomatoes. Put into boiling hot water for about 30 seconds. The peel should come off now. Peel, cut in half and seed. Dice the tomatoes coarsely. Reserve.

2 Heat the wok and add 4 tablespoons oil. Stir-fry the carrots, leek, kohlrabi and broccoli in the wok until just tender. Season with salt and pepper and pour the stock over. Reserve.

3 Dice the tofu, peel the garlic and chop. Heat the remaining oil with the garlic, add the diced tofu and fry until golden brown. Mix the tomatoes and snow peas into the vegetables, sprinkle with diced tofu and serve.

Stir-fried White Cabbage
with Pineapple and Peppers

Ingredients

1 1/4 pounds white cabbage

1 red bell pepper · 7 ounces

pineapple · 1 stalk lemongrass

1 green chili pepper

7 ounces mung bean sprouts

2 tablespoons light soy sauce

4 tablespoons sherry

1 teaspoon chili sauce · salt

1/2 teaspoon Sichuan pepper

1 teaspoon cornstarch

2 tablespoons flaked coconut

1 tablespoon white sesame seeds

1/2 teaspoon grated lemon peel

4 tablespoons vegetable oil

Preparation

SERVES 4

1 Prepare the cabbage and bell pepper, wash and cut into thin strips. Peel the pineapple, remove the core and cut the flesh into chunks. Prepare the lemongrass, wash and chop. Cut the chili pepper in half lengthwise, seed, wash and cut into thin strips. Rinse the mung bean sprouts in a sieve and allow to drain.

2 Mix the soy sauce, sherry, chili sauce, salt, pepper and cornstarch together to make a smooth sauce.

3 Fry the coconut and the sesame seeds in the wok without any oil. Remove and mix with the lemon peel.

4 Heat the oil in the preheated wok. Fry the cabbage and bell pepper until just tender, stirring constantly. Add the pineapple, lemongrass, chili pepper and sprouts and stir in the sauce. Cook for about 2 minutes and sprinkle with the sesame-coconut mixture before serving.

Sweet and Sour Vegetables
with Pineapple and Ginger

*Opposites attract: Gently balancing the flavor extremes of
sweetness and sourness gives this Asian dish its lasting appeal*

Ingredients

3 1/2 ounces Chinese cabbage

4 1/2 ounces carrots

4 1/2 ounces shiitake
mushrooms

4 1/2 ounces snow peas

1 1/4 ounces ginger

2 garlic cloves

2 red chili peppers

3 1/2 ounces bamboo shoots
(canned)

5 ounces pineapple

4 tablespoons vegetable oil

4 tablespoons rice vinegar

4 tablespoons soy sauce

4 tablespoons sweet sherry

2 tablespoons sugar

3/4 cup chicken stock

1 level teaspoon cornstarch

Preparation

SERVES 4

1 Wash the Chinese cabbage and shake dry, cut the leaves in half lengthwise and then into $2/3$-inch strips. Peel the carrots and cut into thin slices. Rub the mushrooms clean and cut in half, quarter large mushrooms. Wash the snow peas and cut in half.

2 Peel the ginger and cut into fine slices. Peel the garlic and chop finely. Cut the chili peppers in half lengthwise, seed, wash and cut into thin slices.

3 Allow the bamboo shoots to drain in a sieve. Peel the pineapple, remove the core and cut the flesh into chunks.

4 Heat the wok and add the oil. Sear the carrots and mushrooms in the oil, then add the Chinese cabbage and snow peas and stir-fry biefly. Add the bamboo shoots, pineapple, vinegar, soy sauce, sherry and sugar. Pour in three quarters of the stock and mix well.

5 Stir the cornstarch with the remaining stock and mix into the vegetables. Simmer everything for another 2 minutes, serve immediately.

Tip

You can use apple vinegar instead of rice vinegar. However, since this is slightly more acid, you should only use 2 tablespoons vinegar. For greater authenticity, substitute rice wine for sherry.

Wok Vegetables
with Snow Peas

Fire, smoke and vegetables: The intense flavor of a
well-cooked stir-fry first tantalizes, then satisfies the taste buds

Ingredients

2 tablespoons dried tree ear
mushrooms

2 tablespoons light soy sauce

2 tablespoons rice wine

scant 1/4 cup vegetable stock

1/2 head Chinese cabbage

1 red bell pepper

1 small zucchini

3 1/2 ounces fresh mushrooms

3 1/2 ounces snow peas

3 1/2 ounces bean sprouts

7 ounces baby corncobs
(canned)

1 garlic clove

1 piece fresh ginger root
(size of a hazelnut)

3 tablespoons peanut oil

1 tablespoon sesame oil

salt · freshly ground pepper

Preparation

SERVES 4

1 Cover the tree ear mushrooms in a small bowl with hot water and allow to swell for about 15 minutes. In another bowl, mix the soy sauce with the rice wine and the stock.

2 Prepare and wash the vegetables. Cut the Chinese cabbage, bell peppers and zucchini into strips. Prepare the mushrooms, rub clean with paper towels and slice. Rinse the snow peas and the bean sprouts with hot water in a sieve and allow to drain. Allow the corncobs to drain and cut in half lengthwise.

3 Pour the tree ear mushrooms into a sieve, rinse briefly, squeeze and cut up small. Peel garlic and ginger and dice both finely.

4 Heat the wok. Add the peanut oil and the sesame oil and heat. Briefly sear the garlic and ginger in the oil. Add the strips of pepper, zucchini, corncobs and the tree ear mushrooms and sear for about 3 minutes, stirring constantly.

5 Then add the fresh mushrooms, snow peas, Chinese cabbage and bean sprouts and cook everything for another 2 minutes, again stirring constantly. Pour in the soy sauce and rice wine mixture. Bring to a boil and continue to cook until the vegetables are tender but still firm to the bite. Season to taste with salt and pepper. Best served with fine basmati rice.

Wok Vegetables
with Cauliflower

Ingredients

1 red and 1 green bell pepper

1 pound carrots · 1 small cauli-

flower · 3 thin leeks

6 baby corncobs (canned)

1 red chili pepper · 1 piece fresh

ginger root (size of a walnut)

2 tablespoons each soy sauce

and rice vinegar

4 tablespoons tomato purée

2 tablespoons brown sugar

1/4 teaspoon each ground cumin

and coriander seeds

1/2 tablespoon cornstarch

1/2 cup vegetable stock

3 tablespoons vegetable oil

Preparation
SERVES 4

1 Prepare the bell peppers, wash and cut into strips. Peel the carrots and cut into strips. Prepare the cauliflower, wash and separate into flowerets, cut the stem into slices. Prepare the leek, wash and cut into strips. Allow the corncobs to drain in a sieve.

2 Cut the chili peppers in half lengthwise, seed, wash and chop finely. Peel the ginger and also chop finely.

3 Mix the soy sauce with the vinegar, tomato purée and sugar. Add the chili pepper, ginger, cumin and coriander. Mix the cornstarch with the stock until smooth and pour into the soy sauce mixture.

4 Heat the oil in the preheated wok. Fry the carrots and cauliflower in the oil for about 3 minutes, stirring constantly. Add the leeks, bell peppers and corncobs and roast for another 2 minutes. Pour the sauce over and allow all to simmer for about 5 minutes until the vegetables are tender but firm to the bite. Serve with basmati rice.

Vegetable Stir-fry
with Baby Corncobs

Ingredients

¾ cup basmati rice · salt · 1 teaspoon vegetable oil · 3 bell peppers (red, yellow, green) · 6 baby corncobs (canned) · ¾ cup green beans · 1 onion · 4 small Thai eggplants · ⅓ cup chickpeas (canned) · ⅔ cup bean sprouts 2 scallions · 2 red chili peppers 2 garlic cloves · 1 piece fresh ginger root (size of a hazelnut) 1 teaspoon ground turmeric 8 tablespoons peanut oil ½ cup vegetable stock 5 tablespoons light soy sauce freshly ground pepper

Preparation
SERVES 4

1 Wash the basmati rice in a sieve, bring to a boil in a pan with about ⅔ cup water, a pinch of salt and 1 teaspoon vegetable oil. Allow to swell for about 15 minutes over low heat.

2 Prepare the bell peppers, wash and cut into strips. Allow the corncobs to drain, then cut in half lengthwise. Prepare the beans, wash and cut into chunks. Peel the onion and cut into eighths lengthwise. Prepare the eggplants, wash and quarter. Rinse the chickpeas and sprouts and allow to drain.

3 Prepare the scallions, wash and cut into rings. For the spice mixture, cut the chili peppers in half lengthwise, seed, wash and chop finely. Peel the garlic and ginger and also chop finely. Mix with the ground cumin.

4 Heat the wok, add 4 tablespoons peanut oil. Fry the vegetables in the wok until tender, then remove. Heat the remaining oil, add the rice and stir-fry for 5 minutes. Add the spice mixture and sear briefly. Add the vegetables and the stock. Season to taste with soy sauce, salt and pepper and mix well.

Broccoli
with Shiitake Mushrooms

Perfect partners: Broccoli and aromatic mushrooms joined together in a wok become a very popular Asian delicacy

Ingredients

12 dried shiitake mushrooms

3 tablespoons soy sauce

salt

1 tablespoons dry sherry

1 teaspoon cornstarch

1 teaspoon sugar

about 2 cups vegetable stock

9 ounces broccoli

1 tablespoon sesame oil

2 tablespoons vegetable oil

1 piece fresh ginger root

(size of a hazelnut)

Preparation

SERVES 4

1 Cover the mushrooms with hot water and allow to swell for about 20 minutes. Drain the mushrooms in a sieve and rinse briefly. Remove the stems and squeeze dry. Cut into pieces.

2 Mix the soy sauce with $1/2$ teaspoon salt, sherry, cornstarch, sugar and stock in a small bowl, then bring to a boil in the wok. Add the mushrooms and simmer for 10 minutes over low heat until the sauce thickens. If the sauce becomes too thick, add a little stock. Reserve.

3 Meanwhile prepare the broccoli, wash and cut into flowerets. Peel the stems and cut diagonally into slices $1/2$-inch thick. Blanch the stems in boiling hot for 2 minutes, the flowerets for 1 minute. Rinse the broccoli under cold water, then allow to drain well in a sieve.

4 Put the mushrooms and sauce on a plate and keep warm.

5 Heat the wok and pour in the sesame and vegetable oil. Peel the ginger, chop and sear in the hot oil. Add the broccoli and fry for 2 minutes, stirring constantly. Add the mushrooms and the sauce, stir and serve very hot.

Vegetable Pot
with Coconut and Bamboo

Absolute seduction: This pot with ginger, lemongrass and lime leaves brings together the most enchanting aromas of Asian cuisine

Ingredients

2/3 cup basmati rice · salt

3 tablespoons vegetable oil

5 ounces tofu · 1 garlic clove

1 onion

1 piece fresh ginger root

(size of a walnut)

1 stalk lemongrass

5-6 small Thai eggplants

(or 1 large eggplant)

2 ounces each enoki mush-

rooms and button mushrooms

1 zucchini

1 red chili pepper

2 ounces bamboo shoots

(canned) · 3 lime leaves

1/4 cup unsweetened coconut

milk

1 1/4 cup vegetable stock

juice of 1 lime

2 teaspoons soy sauce

Preparation

SERVES 4

1 Rinse the basmati rice in a sieve under running cold water until the water runs clear. Fill the rice into a pan and cover with 1 1/2 cup cold water. Add a pinch of salt and 1 teaspoon oil, stir and bring to a boil. Allow to swell for about 15 minutes over low heat. Keep warm.

2 Rinse the tofu, pat dry and cut coarsely into pieces. Peel the garlic, onion and ginger and chop finely. Prepare the lemongrass and cut into pieces.

3 Prepare, wash and slice the Thai eggplants (or cut the large eggplant into small pieces). Rub the mushrooms clean with paper towels, cut the button mushrooms in half. Prepare the zucchini, wash and cut in half lengthwise, then slice. Cut the chili pepper in half lengthwise, seed, wash and cut into rings. Allow the bamboo shoots to drain in a sieve.

4 Heat the wok, add the remaining oil and roast the tofu until golden. Add the garlic, onion, ginger, lemongrass, chili and lime leaves and fry all together briefly. Then add the eggplants, mushrooms, zucchini slices and bean sprouts and cook everything together briefly. Pour in the coconut milk and stock and allow to simmer for 6 minutes.

5 Season the vegetable pot well with lime juice and soy sauce. Remove the lemongrass and lime leaves. Fill into small bowls and serve with the basmati rice.

Mandarin Pancakes
with Wok Vegetables

Ingredients

2 1/2 cups all-purpose flour

about 6 teaspoons vegetable oil

1 piece fresh ginger root (size of

a hazelnut) · 2 garlic cloves

9 ounces carrots · 1/2 pound scal-

lions · 1/2 pound celery

4 1/4 ounces baby corncobs

(canned) · 1 ounce alfalfa sprouts

2 tablespoons sesame oil

1 tablespoon vegetable oil

2 tablespoons hoisin sauce

6 tablespoons light soy sauce

3/4 cup vegetable stock

1 tablespoon hot chili bean paste

(or sambal oelek)

Preparation
SERVES 4

1 For the pancakes, knead a smooth dough with the flour, 3/4 cup water and 2 teaspoons oil and form into a ball. Cover and leave to rest for one hour.

2 Peel and chop the ginger and garlic. Peel the carrots, prepare scallions and wash. Cut into 2-inches strips. Prepare the celery and wash. Slice the stalks, cut the green into strips. Rinse the corncobs and sprouts in a sieve, then allow to drain. Cut the corncobs in half lengthwise.

3 Knead the dough, divide into 16 portions, press each flat and brush one side with oil. Bring 2 pancakes together, oil sides facing, and roll out. Fry the pancakes, one by one, in a pan without oil. Turn when bubbles appear, continue frying for another 2 minutes. Allow to cool. Pull apart at the edges and loosely fold in half.

4 Heat all the oil in the wok. Fry the vegetables with the garlic and ginger – without the sprouts – for 3 minutes. Add the hoisin and soy sauce, stock and bean paste and simmer together. Fill the pancakes with celery green, vegetables and sprouts and roll up.

Chili Cauliflower
with Leek and Tomatoes

Ingredients

1 white onion

4 red chili peppers

4 garlic cloves

1 piece fresh ginger root

(size of a walnut)

9 ounces leek

1 cauliflower (about 2 pounds)

salt · 1/2 pound tomatoes

4 tablespoons coconut oil

1/2 teaspoon ground cumin

3 tablespoons light soy sauce

3 tablespoons sweet soy sauce

(ketjap manis)

Preparation

SERVES 4

1 Peel the onion and dice finely. Cut the chili peppers in half lengthwise, seed, wash and cut into thin strips. Peel the garlic and ginger and chop both finely.

2 Trim and wash the cauliflower. Cut the cleaned leek into thin 2-inch strips. Separate the cauliflower into flowerets, cut larger flowerets into two lengthwise. Cook the cauliflower flowerets in boiling salted water for about 4 minutes until tender, pour into a sieve, rinse under cold running water and allow to drain.

3 Cut an X into the top and bottom of the tomatoes. Put into boiling hot water for 30 seconds. The skin should come off now. Peel, cut in half, seed, and dice the flesh.

4 Heat the wok and pour in the coconut oil. Add the onion, chili, garlic and ginger and sear over medium heat. Add the cumin, the cauliflower flowerets and the strips of leek and cook everything together for 2 minutes.

5 Mix both soy sauces with 3/4 cup water, pour into the vegetable dish and simmer for 2 minutes. Add the diced tomatoes and heat everything briefly once more.

Stir-fried Savoy Cabbage
with Coconut

A touch of the exotic: Fresh coconut, hot red chili and
lemon ensure that this dish is one your palate will savor

Ingredients

2 pounds savoy cabbage

2 onions

1 garlic clove

1 red chili pepper

3 tablespoons vegetable oil

1 $^2/_3$ cup unsweetened
coconut milk

$^1/_2$ teaspoon grated lemon
rind

salt · freshly ground pepper

2 ounces fresh coconut flesh
(or flaked coconut)

Preparation
SERVES 4

1 Prepare the cabbage, wash the leaves and shred coarsely. Peel the onions and garlic and chop finely. Cut the chili peppers in half lengthwise, seed, wash and cut into thin strips.

2 Heat the oil in the preheated wok. Fry the shredded cabbage for 5 minutes, stirring constantly. Add the onions, garlic and chili and fry for another 5 minutes.

3 Add the coconut milk and the lemon rind. Season the vegetables to taste with salt. Cook the vegetables over medium heat until tender, stirring occasionally.

4 Season the vegetables to taste once more with salt and pepper. Thinly slice the coconut flesh with a potato peeler. Garnish the vegetable dish with thinly shaved coconut strips and serve.

Tip

To open a coconut, first open two of the three "eyes" with a hammer and nail. Allow the coconut water to run out. Make a small incision with a saw and tap open with a hammer.

Noodles
and Rice

Rice Noodles
with Leek and Peanuts

Noodles are immensely popular in Asia – so it's no surprise
that there are many delicious Wok recipes involving noodles

Ingredients

¹/₄ pound wide rice noodles

¹/₂ pound carrots

10 ¹/₂ ounces leek

1 garlic clove

1 piece fresh ginger root

(size of a hazelnut)

3 tablespoons vegetable oil

2 tablespoons roasted salted

peanuts

salt · freshly ground pepper

Preparation

SERVES 4

1 Cover the rice noodles in a bowl with boiling water and leave for about 15 minutes to swell until they are soft but still firm to the bite. Allow the noodles to drain in a sieve.

2 Prepare the carrots and leek, wash, then cut into thin, long strips. Peel the garlic and ginger, chop both finely.

3 Heat the oil in the preheated wok. Sear the ginger and garlic. Add the strips of carrot and leek, and fry, stirring constantly.

4 Add the drained noodles to the wok together with the peanuts and fry everything together for about another 2 minutes, stirring constantly. Finally season to taste with salt and pepper.

Tip

Vegetable "noodles" are very decorative and easy to make: Simply sliver carrots very thinly with a potato peeler or sharp knife. Cut the leek into thin strips with a knife.

Noodles
with Mushrooms

Lovers of Asian cuisine will definitely want another helping of this noodle dish with four varieties of mushrooms

Ingredients

10 dried tree ear mushrooms

1/2 pound button mushrooms

1/2 pound oyster mushrooms

1 3/4 ounces shiitake mushrooms

1/4 pound soy bean sprouts

1 carrot · 1 scallion

2 garlic cloves

1 piece fresh ginger root (size of a hazelnut)

6 ounces Chinese cabbage

1 tablespoon cornstarch

4 tablespoons rice wine

14 ounces narrow noodles

salt

3 tablespoons vegetable oil

2/3 cup vegetable stock

3 tablespoons soy sauce

freshly ground pepper

Preparation

SERVES 4

1 Soak the dried tree ear mushrooms in hot water and leave to swell for about 15 minutes. Then wash them, squeeze dry, remove the hard stalks and cut the rest into strips. Prepare the three fresh mushroom varieties and rub clean with paper towels. Remove the hard stalks from the shiitake mushrooms and cut all fresh mushrooms into thin slices. Rinse the bean sprouts in a sieve under hot running water and allow to drain.

2 Peel the carrot and cut into matchstick-size strips. Prepare the scallion, wash and cut into fine rings. Peel the garlic and ginger, chop both finely. Prepare the Chinese cabbage, wash and cut into thin strips. In a cup or small bowl, stir the cornstarch with the rice wine until smooth.

3 Cook the noodles in plenty of boiling salted water according to the instructions on the package. Meanwhile, heat the oil in the preheated wok. Add the scallion, garlic and ginger and sear, stirring constantly. Add the mushrooms and carrot and fry all for about 2 minutes.

4 Stir in the bean sprouts and Chinese cabbage and fry together for 1 minute. Add the rice wine with the cornstarch, the stock and soy sauce, bring to a boil and season to taste with salt and pepper.

5 Drain the noodles in a sieve and mix with the mushroom sauce. Garnish with chopped parsley (optional) and serve.

Rice Noodles
with Savoy Cabbage

Grab your chopsticks, get set, go! The rice noodles, mushrooms and colorful vegetables bring the Far Eastern quality of life to your table

Ingredients

10 1/2 ounces wide rice noodles

9 ounces savoy cabbage

10 1/2 ounces oyster mushrooms

1/2 red bell pepper

1/3 cup vegetable stock

3 tablespoons lime juice

3 tablespoons light soy sauce

4 tablespoons vegetable oil

salt

cayenne pepper

a few cilantro or chervil leaves

Preparation

SERVES 4

1 Cover the rice noodles in a bowl with boiling water and allow to swell for about 15 minutes, until they are soft but still firm to the bite. Then allow to drain in a sieve.

2 Meanwhile prepare the cabbage, remove the thick ribs on the leaves, wash and shred finely. Prepare the mushrooms, rub clean with paper towels and slice finely. Prepare the half bell pepper, wash, seed and dice as finely as possible.

3 Stir the stock together with the lime juice and the soy sauce in a small bowl.

4 Heat the oil in the preheated wok. Fry the mushrooms in the hot oil for about 1 minute, stirring constantly, then move them to the edge. Add the cabbage and fry for 4-5 minutes, stirring constantly, until it is soft but firm to the bite.

5 Stir the mushrooms back in, add the drained rice noodles and sauce mixture and heat everything together briefly, stirring constantly. Season to taste with salt and cayenne pepper, sprinkle with the diced bell pepper and herb leaves, and serve.

Tip

Rice noodles come in many different varieties in Asian shops. These are not cooked, but simply soaked in hot water. Alternately, you can also use Italian pasta.

Egg Noodles
with Cabbage and Mushrooms

Ingredients

1/2 pound Chinese egg noodles

salt

1 pound white cabbage

1 large carrot

1/2 pound shiitake mushrooms

4 tablespoons peanut oil

freshly ground pepper

1 teaspoon Chinese five-spice powder

4 tablespoons soy sauce

Preparation

SERVES 4

1 Cook the egg noodles in plenty of boiling salted water according to the instructions on the package. Pour into a sieve, rinse with cold water and allow to drain.

2 Quarter the cabbage, remove the trunk, then shred each quarter into thin strips crosswise. Wash the cabbage and allow to drain.

3 Peel the carrot. Cut into thin slices lengthwise, then into thin strips. Prepare the mushrooms, rub clean with paper towels and cut in half.

4 Heat the wok, add half the oil and stir-fry the cabbage and carrot over medium heat, stirring constantly. Under no circumstances should they brown. Remove the vegetables. Heat the remaining oil in the wok, add the mushrooms and fry over high heat until golden brown.

5 Add the strips of vegetables and the noodles to the wok. Mix everything together well, season with salt, pepper, five-spice powder and soy sauce. Serve immediately.

Glass Noodles
with Vegetables and Sesame

Ingredients

½ pound glass noodles

2 carrots · 1 yellow bell pepper

1 medium zucchini

1 red chili pepper

1 garlic clove

4 tablespoons sesame oil

salt · freshly ground pepper

1 cup soy bean sprouts

2 tablespoons soy sauce

1 tablespoon oyster sauce

1 tablespoon chopped cilantro
leaves

1 tablespoon white sesame seeds

Preparation

SERVES 4

1 Cover the noodles in a bowl with tepid water and allow to swell for about 10 minutes.

2 Peel the carrots. Prepare the bell pepper, cut in half lengthwise, seed and wash. Prepare and wash the zucchini. Cut the carrots, peppers and zucchini into thin strips. Cut the chili pepper in half lengthwise, seed, wash and chop finely. Peel the garlic and also chop finely.

3 Heat the wok and add 3 tablespoons oil. Add the garlic and fry until golden brown. Add the vegetables and fry, stirring constantly, but do not allow to brown. Season with salt and pepper.

4 Allow the noodles to drain. With scissors, cut into small pieces and stir into the vegetables. Rinse the bean sprouts under hot running water and allow to drain. Add the soy sauce, oyster sauce, remaining oil and sprouts to the vegetables. Garnish with cilantro leaves, sprinkle with sesame seeds and serve.

Egg Noodles
with Asparagus and Tamarind

One of the best trios ever: When lemongrass, asparagus and
tamarind join forces, noodle fans are sure of something exquisite

Ingredients

¹/₄ pound Chinese egg noodles

salt

¹/₄ pound tofu

¹/₂ pound green asparagus

1 small head bok choy

1 shallot

1 garlic clove

2 potatoes

1 stalk lemongrass

1 tablespoon tamarind paste

1 tablespoon vegetable oil

2 lime leaves

2 teaspoons sambal ketjap

1 tablespoon soy sauce

Preparation

SERVES 4

1 Cook the egg noodles in plenty of boiling salted water to the imstructions on the package until tender but firm to the bite. Pour into a sieve, rinse with cold water and allow to drain.

2 Rinse the tofu, pat dry and dice. Peel the lower third of the asparagus, wash and cut into pieces. Prepare the bok choy, wash and cut into small strips. Peel the shallot and garlic and chop finely. Peel the potatoes and dice. Prepare the lemongrass and cut into pieces. Dissolve the tamarind paste in 3 tablespoons warm water.

3 Heat the oil in the preheated wok. Sear the garlic, shallot and diced potato for about 5 minutes. Add ¹/₂ cup water, the lime leaves, diluted tamarind paste and lemongrass. Cover and allow to cook for about 10 minutes.

4 Remove the lid, add the asparagus and bok choy and cook for about 5 minutes. Add the diced tofu and fry for about 2 minutes. Stir in the noodles, season to taste with sambal ketjap and soy sauce, and serve.

Tip

Like the ever-popular sambal oelek, sambal ketjap is a Chinese seasoning made with chili peppers. It gets it characteristic flavor from fermented soy beans.

Egg Noodles
with Beef and Swiss Chard

This will definitely keep you satisfied: This delicious noodle dish with meat and chard could make Italian pasta chefs green with envy

Ingredients

1/2 pound Chinese egg noodles

salt · 10 ounces beef

(for stir-frying)

1 red chili pepper

3 garlic cloves

3 large Swiss chard leaves

4 tablespoons vegetable oil

1 teaspoon mustard seeds

2 cups vegetable stock

3 tablespoons soy sauce

freshly ground pepper

Preparation

SERVES 4

1 Cook the egg noodles in plenty of boiling salted water according to the instructions on the package until tender but firm to the bite. Pour into a sieve, rinse with cold water and allow to drain. Reserve. Keep warm.

2 Cut the meat into thin, bite-size pieces. Cut the chili peppers in half lengthwise, seed, wash and chop finely. Peel the garlic and cut into slices. Prepare and wash the chard leaves. Remove the white stem and cut it into 1/2-inch pieces, shred the green coarsely.

3 Heat the oil in the preheated wok. Fry the mustard seeds, garlic and chili, then add the white of the chard and the meat and fry briefly over low heat, but do not allow to brown. Add the stock and soy sauce, cover and cook for 3 minutes. Then add the green chard strips, cover and cook for another 7 minutes until done. Season with salt and pepper. Stir the noodles in and heat.

Tip

For variation, try broccoli, bell peppers or savoy cabbage instead of the Swiss chard. Give the dish extra "bite" by adding lightly roasted cashew nuts or peanuts.

Chinese Egg Noodles
with Chicken and Shrimp

Ingredients

¾ pound Chinese egg noodles

salt

1 bunch scallions

2 garlic cloves

¾ pound skinless, boneless chicken breast portions

1 chili pepper

4 tablespoons vegetable oil

¼ pound peeled shrimp (ready-to-cook)

½ cup bean sprouts

1 tablespoon grated fresh ginger

4 tablespoons soy sauce

Preparation

SERVES 4

1 Cook the egg noodles in plenty of boiling salted water according to the instructions on the package until tender but firm to the bite. Pour into a sieve, rinse with cold water and allow to drain.

2 Prepare the scallions, wash and cut into slices. Peel the garlic and chop finely. Wash the chicken breast, pat dry and cut first into slices, then into strips. Cut the chili pepper in half lengthwise, seed, wash and chop very finely.

3 Heat the oil in the preheated wok. Sear the prepared ingredients, stirring constantly: First add the meat and stir-fry, then add the shrimp and also fry. Finally add the garlic and scallions, with the chili pepper at the end.

4 Rinse the soy sprouts in a sieve under hot running water and allow to drain. Add to the wok with the ginger, soy sauce and noodles and mix everything together lightly.

Indonesian Style Noodles
with Pork

Ingredients

½ pound Chinese egg noodles

salt

1 small head Chinese cabbage

¼ pound shiitake mushrooms

⅔ pound pork tenderloin

1 red chili pepper

1 stalk lemongrass

3 tablespoons vegetable oil

1 tablespoon fresh grated ginger

½ teaspoon Chinese five-spice
powder (or other Chinese
spice mixture)

2 tablespoons rice wine

4 tablespoons soy sauce

Preparation

SERVES 4

1 Cook the egg noodles in plenty of boiling salted water according to the instructions on the package until tender but firm to the bite. Pour into a sieve, rinse with cold water and allow to drain.

2 Prepare the Chinese cabbage, wash and shred into ½-inch strips. Rub the shiitake mushrooms clean with paper towels. Cut the mushrooms and the pork into thin slices.

3 Cut the chili peppers in half lengthwise, seed, wash and chop finely. Prepare the lemongrass, wash and cut into pieces.

4 Heat the oil in the preheated wok. First sear the meat, then the mushrooms and the cabbage. Add the chili pepper, lemongrass, ginger and spices. Pour in the rice wine and soy sauce. Stir in the noodles and allow to simmer for about 3 minutes. Then serve.

Tofu Noodle Bake
with Water Chestnuts

Fancy something really different? Egg noodles with tofu, sweet potatoes and water chestnuts will tempt any connoisseur's palate

Ingredients

5 ounces Chinese egg noodles

salt

2 sweet potatoes

3 scallions

1 onion

1 garlic clove

1 red chili pepper

1/4 pound smoked tofu

2 teaspoons sesame oil

2 ounces water chestnuts (canned)

1/4 cup vegetable stock

2 tomatoes

2 tablespoons soy sauce

freshly ground pepper

1/2 bunch chives

Preparation

SERVES 4

1 Cook the egg noodles in plenty of boiling salted water according to the instructions on the package until tender but firm to the bite. Pour into a sieve, rinse with cold water and allow to drain. Reserve and keep warm.

2 Peel the sweet potatoes, wash and dice small. Prepare the scallions, wash and cut into pieces. Peel the onion and garlic, chop both very finely. Cut the chili pepper in half lengthwise, seed, wash and cut into strips. Cut the tofu into strips.

3 Heat the oil in the preheated wok. Sear the tofu strips briefly, then remove. Sear the onions, garlic and chili pepper in the remaining oil. Add the sweet potato, scallions and drained chestnuts and cook for about 5 minutes. Pour in the vegetable stock, cover and cook for another 15 minutes.

4 Wash the tomatoes and cut into segments, removing the stalk. Add noodles, tofu and tomatoes to the vegetables and fry for 5 minutes. Season to taste with soy sauce and pepper. Wash the chives, shake dry and cut into rolls. Sprinkle the noodle dish with the chives.

Tip

For variation, use chicken breast instead of tofu. In that case, mix 1 teaspoon sesame oil with 1 tablespoon soy sauce. Allow the meat to marinate for 15 minutes, then pat dry and fry.

Indonesian Fried Rice
with Chicken Breast

*Nasi goreng is a rice specialty to get hooked on: It is usually
served with shredded omelette and prawn crackers on top*

Ingredients

½ pound skinless, boneless
chicken breast portions

1 tablespoon honey

3 tablespoons soy sauce

2 tablespoons curry powder

1 tablespoon ketchup

1 teaspoon cornstarch

2 stalks lemongrass

1 bunch scallions

1 red bell pepper

2 garlic cloves

1 red chili pepper

4 tablespoons sesame oil

4 cups cooked basmati rice

Preparation

SERVES 4

1 Rinse the chicken in cold water, pat dry and cut into fine strips. Make a marinade by stirring together the honey, soy sauce, 1 tablespoon of the curry powder, ketchup and corn-starch. Add the meat to the marinade and leave to stand for 15 minutes.

2 Wash the lemongrass, cut in half lengthways and slice into fine rings. Trim and wash the scallions and cut into pieces ½-inch to ¼-inch long. Prepare and wash the pepper and dice finely.

3 Peel the garlic and chop finely. Wash the chili, remove the seeds and cut into very fine strips.

4 Heat the oil in the preheated wok. Stir-fry the meat. Add the onions, pepper and lemongrass and briefly fry. Stir in the garlic and chili. Add the cold rice and stir-fry together for about 3 minutes. Finally add the remaining curry powder and give it a good stir. Cook for one more minute.

Tip

Don't feel like meat? Curry rice can become a vegetarian meal if, instead of chicken, plantains or bananas find their way into the wok. In that case, use only half the marinade and stir-fry very briefly.

Coconut Curry Rice
with Snow Peas

Ingredients

1 pound snow peas

1 bunch scallions

1 yellow bell pepper

1 onion

1 garlic clove

1 piece fresh ginger root (size of

a hazelnut)

2 tablespoons vegetable oil

2 cups long-grain rice

1 ²/₃ cups unsweetened coconut

milk

1 cup vegetable stock

2 tablespoons lemon juice

2 teaspoons curry powder

salt · 1 small bunch basil

Preparation

SERVES 4

1 Prepare the snow peas and wash. Prepare the scallions, wash and cut in fine rings together with the green. Prepare the bell pepper, wash and cut into strips. Peel the onion, garlic and ginger and chop all finely.

2 Heat the oil in the preheated wok. Stir-fry the snow peas, scallions and bell pepper for 2 minutes over high heat, stirring constantly, then remove. Add the onion, garlic and ginger to the wok and fry for one minute. Add the rice, stir in and also fry until translucent.

3 Pour in the coconut milk and stock. Season the rice to taste with lemon juice, curry powder and salt, cover and cook for about 15 minutes until done.

4 Stir in the stir-fried vegetables and cook for another 5 minutes until done. Wash the basil and shake dry, pluck the leaves from the stems and chop coarsely. Sprinkle the basil over the curry coconut rice and serve.

Egg Curry Rice
with Colorful Vegetables

Ingredients

1 ²/₃ cups basmati rice

1 small carrot

1 thin leek

1 red bell pepper

¹/₄ pound mushrooms

¹/₄ pound soy bean sprouts

4 tablespoons vegetable oil

¹/₄ pound peas (frozen)

2 teaspoons curry powder

salt · 2 eggs

2 tablespoons rice wine

freshly ground pepper

Preparation

SERVES 4

1 Rinse the rice thoroughly under running water. Bring to a boil in a pan with 3 ¹/₂ cups water, cover, lower the heat and simmer for about 20 minutes. Drain off excess water and allow the rice to cool.

2 Peel the carrot and dice finely. Trim the leek, wash and cut into strips crosswise. Prepare and wash the pepper, then dice. Rub the mushrooms clean, cut into slices. Rinse the bean sprouts in a sieve under hot running water and allow to drain.

3 Heat the wok, add 3 tablespoons of oil and heat. Add the rice and fry until crisp, stirring constantly.

4 Remove the rice from the wok, then heat the remaining oil. Add the vegetables and fry for 5 minutes. Stir in the peas and curry powder, salt and fry for another minute. Add the rice again. Stir the eggs with the rice wine, salt and pepper in an extra bowl, pour into the wok and stir briefly until the eggs have set, but are not too dry.

Nasi Goreng
with Fried Eggs

In Asia, they serve fried rice for breakfast.

In America, we will rather have it for brunch or for dinner

Ingredients

2 cups long-grain rice

salt

1 bunch scallions

3/4 pound pork tenderloin

4 shallots

2 garlic cloves

6 tablespoons vegetable oil

4 eggs

freshly ground pepper

2 tablespoons sweet soy sauce
(kecap manis)

1 teaspoon sambal oelek

1/4 teaspoon ground galangal

Preparation

SERVES 4

1 Rinse the rice under running water and allow to drain. Bring to a boil in a pan with 3 cups water and 1 teaspoon salt, cover, lower the heat and allow to swell for about 20 minutes. Fluff up the rice, remove the lid and switch off the heat when the remaining water has evaporated. Allow to cool.

2 Prepare and wash the scallions. Quarter the white ends lengthwise, then cut crosswise into pieces about 1 1/2-inches long. Cut the meat first into slices, then into strips. Peel the shallots and cut into fine slices. Peel and chop the garlic finely.

3 Heat 3 tablespoons oil in the preheated wok. Open half the shallots to form rings and fry until golden brown and crisp, stirring constantly. Remove the roasted shallots and allow to drain on paper towels. Add 2 tablespoons oil to the wok and fry the meat for about 5 minutes until crisp, stirring constantly.

4 Add the remaining shallots, garlic and scallions and fry briefly. Finally add the rice and fry for 3-5 minutes over high heat, stirring constantly until golden yellow. Meanwhile heat 1 tablespoon oil in a pan and fry the eggs, season the egg white lightly with salt and pepper.

5 Mix the fried rice with ketjap manis, sambal oelek and galangal, season to taste well with salt and pepper and arrange on plates. Arrange one fried egg on each portion of nasi goreng and sprinkle with the roasted shallots before serving.

Fried Rice
with Cashew Nuts

A mixture that has it all: Peppers, scallions and crunchy cashew nuts ensure this dish has plenty of bite and flavor

Ingredients

salt

1 ²/₃ cups long-grain rice

1 each small red, yellow and green bell pepper

4 ounces cucumber

2 scallions

4 ounces cashew nuts

4 tablespoons oil

freshly ground pepper

Preparation

SERVES 4

1 Bring 4 cups water to a boil, salt lightly, add the rice and stir once. Bring the rice to a boil and allow to swell for about 20 minutes. Allow the rice to cool.

2 Prepare the peppers, wash and dice finely. Wash the cucumber and also dice finely. Trim the scallions, wash and cut into fine rings.

3 Heat the wok. Fry the cashew nuts without any oil, remove and set aside. Add the oil to the wok and heat. Add the bell peppers, cucumber and onions and sear briefly. Add the rice and nuts, stir well and continue frying for 3 minutes.

4 Season the fried rice with salt and pepper, continue to fry for another 2 minutes. Serve on warm plates or in small bowls.

Tip

Make the rice even crunchier by replacing ²/₃ cup long-grain rice with wild rice. This goes particularly well with peanuts or peeled, halved almonds.

Sticky Rice Balls
with Pork Filling

Ingredients

1 cup sticky rice

1/2 pound shrimp
(cooked and peeled)

2 scallions

5 Chinese water chestnuts
(canned)

5 ounces ground pork

1 egg

1 tablespoon potato flour

2 tablespoons fish sauce

freshly ground pepper

2 tablespoons vegetable oil

Preparation
SERVES 4

1 Allow the rice to swell for 8-10 hours in tepid water, then drain and cook for about 20 minutes in a steamer.

2 Rinse the shrimp and chop finely. Trim the scallions, wash and cut into fine rings. Allow the chestnuts to drain and cut into small pieces. Mix the prepared ingredients with the ground pork, egg, potato flour and fish sauce and season to taste with pepper.

3 Shape 2 tablespoons rice into a flat circle. Fill 1 tablespoon meat mixture in the middle and form the rice around to make a small, even ball. Continue to shape rice balls until all ingredients have been used up.

4 Brush the base of a bamboo basket with oil and add the rice balls. Pour about 1/2-inch water into the wok and bring to a boil. Insert the bamboo basket, cover and steam for 15 minutes. Serve the rice balls with chili sauce or vegetables (optional).

Fried Rice Balls
with Spicy Sauce

Ingredients

2 cups long-grain and wild rice
mixture · salt
1 bunch scallions
2 garlic cloves
1 piece fresh ginger root (size of
a hazelnut)
1 cucumber · 2 eggs · 1/3 cup flour
2 tablespoons ground almonds
freshly ground pepper
vegetable oil, for frying
4 ounces sweet chili sauce
2 teaspoons rice vinegar
1 teaspoon soy sauce
a few lettuce leaves

Preparation
SERVES 4

1   Bring the rice to a boil with 2 1/2 cups salted
water, then allow to swell for 20 minutes over
low heat.

2   Meanwhile, prepare the scallions, peel the
garlic and ginger and chop all finely. Peel the
cucumber, cut in half lengthwise, seed and
dice finely. Mix the cooked rice with the eggs,
flour and almonds, season to taste with salt
and pepper. With wet hands, shape mixture
into walnut-size balls.

3   Heat the wok and add 1 tablespoon oil. Fry the
scallions, garlic and ginger for 2 minutes and
fill into a bowl. Add the diced cucumber and
chili sauce, season to taste with rice vinegar
and soy sauce.

4   Heat the oil and gradually fry the rice balls in
the oil for 4-5 minutes until golden brown.
Wash the lettuce leaves, pat dry and cut into
strips. Serve the rice balls on the lettuce
leaves with the sauce.

Fish and Seafood

Shanghai Style Shrimp
with Glass Noodles

*This is authentic Shanghai cuisine: Ingredients are braised very
slowly to create a rich wok dish which balances textures and aromas*

Ingredients

1 pound shrimp (cooked and
peeled)

2 ounces dried morel
mushrooms

4 garlic cloves

1 dried chili pepper

1/2 pound snow peas

1/2 pound button mushrooms

15 ounces baby corncobs
(canned)

4 ounces tofu

11 ounces glass noodles

4 tablespoons sesame oil

3 tablespoons soy sauce

1 tablespoon freshly grated
ginger

2 tablespoons oyster sauce

salt · freshly ground pepper

Preparation

SERVES 4

1 Rinse the shrimp in a sieve under cold running water and
allow to drain. Pour hot water over the morel mushrooms and
allow to swell for 15 minutes. Allow to drain, then wash well
to remove any remaining sand.

2 Peel the garlic and cut in half. Crush the chili pepper very
finely in a mortar with a pestle. Prepare the snow peas and
wash. Rub the morel mushrooms clean with paper towels and
slice evenly. Allow the corncobs to drain and quarter lengthwise. Wash the tofu, pat dry and dice.

3 Cover the glass noodles with boiling hot water and allow to
stand for 10 minutes to swell. Drain, rinse with warm water
and allow to drain. Reserve and keep warm.

4 Heat the oil in wok. Then add, in this order: the snow peas,
the button mushrooms, garlic and morels. Fry each for about
2 minutes over high heat, stirring constantly, while moving
the previous ingredient to the edge of the wok. Then add the
corncobs, shrimp and diced tofu. Fry all for about 1 minute
over high heat, stirring occasionally.

5 Add the soy sauce, the grated ginger, oyster sauce and crushed
chili pepper. Mix the vegetables with the shrimp and spices,
season to taste with salt and pepper and allow to braise for
about 1 minute. Add the noodles, stir in and serve hot.

Seafood Curry
with Shrimp and Mango

*Indonesian cuisine is rich and varied, reflecting the many
diverse influences which have shaped the country's history*

Ingredients

1 1/4 pounds frozen seafood
(e.g. shrimp, mussels, squid)

2 ripe mangos

3 tablespoons flaked coconut

3 tablespoons unsweetened
coconut milk

1/4 teaspoon chili powder

2 tablespoons curry powder

1 large carrot · 2 onions

3 garlic cloves

2 celery stalks

2 tablespoons oil

juice of 1/2 lemon

5 tablespoons sesame oil

salt · freshly ground pepper

Preparation

SERVES 4

1 Allow the seafood to defrost. Then rinse under cold running water and pat dry with paper towels.

2 Peel the mangoes, cut the flesh from the pit and into slices 1/4-inch thick. Place half the flesh in a food processor with the flaked coconut, coconut milk, chili powder, curry powder and 3 tablespoons water and blend until smooth.

3 Peel the carrot and dice. Peel the onion and garlic and chop finely. Prepare the celery, wash and dice finely. Reserve some of the celery green for the garnish.

4 Heat the wok, add the oil and the diced vegetables. Add the seafood and fry briefly. Stir in the sauce and allow everything to simmer over low heat for about 8 minutes. If the sauce gets too thick, add a little extra coconut milk or water to thin down.

5 Season the seafood curry with lemon juice, sesame oil, salt and pepper and garnish with the remaining mango slices and celery green.

Tip

Instead of a variety of seafood, you could use jumbo shrimp for this dish. They are available frozen, cooked (pink) and fresh (gray) in most markets.

Sweet and Sour Shrimp
with Bell Peppers and Chili

Ingredients

1 egg white

2 tablespoons balsamic vinegar

4 tablespoons rice wine

2 tablespoons soy sauce

1 tablespoon tomato ketchup

salt · freshly ground pepper

20 jumbo shrimp (cooked and peeled)

2 red bell peppers

4 scallions

1 red chili pepper

2 tablespoons cornstarch

5 tablespoons vegetable oil

1/4 teaspoon ground ginger

4 tablespoons lobster stock

Preparation
SERVES 4

1 Whisk the egg white until foamy and stir with the vinegar, rice wine, soy sauce and ketchup to make a marinade. Season with salt and pepper. Rinse the shrimp under cold running water, allow to drain and marinate for 20 minutes.

2 Prepare the bell peppers, wash and cut into 1/2-inch dice. Prepare the scallions, wash and cut into rings. Seed the chili pepper, wash and chop finely.

3 Remove the shrimp from the marinade, allow to drain and dust with cornstarch. Heat the oil in the wok and sear the shrimp, stirring constantly. Remove from the wok and keep warm.

4 Cook the vegetables in the oil for about 5 minutes over medium heat until done. Season with ginger, add the marinade and the lobster stock. Allow to simmer for 3 minutes. Finally stir in the fried shrimp.

Giant Shrimp
in a Coat of Leeks

Ingredients

8 giant shrimp (about 1 ¼
ounces each)

2 sticks of leek

salt

2 garlic cloves

1 piece fresh ginger root
(size of a hazelnut)

½ bunch parsley

1 tablespoon honey

juice of 1 lemon

4 teaspoons dry sherry

4 tablespoons sesame oil

freshly ground pepper

2 limes

Preparation

SERVES 4

1 Peel the shrimp, cut along the back and devein. Rinse the shrimp under cold running water and pat dry with paper towels.

2 Prepare the leek, cut lengthwise and wash thoroughly. Remove eight unblemished leaves, briefly blanch in boiling salted water, rinse under cold running water and allow to drain.

3 For the marinade, peel both garlic and ginger and chop finely. Wash the parsley, shake dry, pluck the leaves from the stems and chop.

Stir the garlic with the ginger and parsley, honey, lemon juice, sherry and 3 tablespoons sesame oil and season with salt and pepper. Add the shrimp and allow to marinate for 20 minutes.

4 Remove the shrimp from the marinade and allow to drain on paper towels. Wrap a leek leaf around each shrimp and fasten with a wooden skewer or toothpick. Heat the wok and add the remaining oil. Cook the shrimp in the wok for about 5 minutes. Sprinkle with sesame seeds and serve on slices of lime.

Stir-fried Shrimp
with Hot Sprouts

As hot as it gets in Asia: Sambal oelek is a hot paste
used as a relish in Indonesian and Malaysian cooking

Ingredients

9 ounces Chinese egg noodles

salt · 1 bunch scallions

1 garlic clove

$^1/_3$ cup soy bean sprouts

16 shrimp (cooked and
peeled)

3 tablespoons vegetable oil

2 tablespoons cornstarch

1 cup vegetable stock

$^1/_2$ teaspoon sambal oelek

1 teaspoon sugar

1 tablespoon lemon juice

2 teaspoons tomato paste

Preparation

SERVES 4

1 Cook the egg noodles in plenty boiling salted water according to the instructions on the package until done. Rinse in a sieve under running cold water, and allow to drain.

2 Prepare the scallions, wash and cut into rings. Peel the garlic and chop finely. Rinse the bean sprouts in a sieve under hot running water and allow to drain. Rinse the shrimp under cold running water and allow to drain.

3 Heat the wok and add 1 tablespoon oil. Fry the noodles in the oil until crisp, remove and keep warm. Add the remaining oil to the wok and sear the shrimp. Add the garlic and fry.

4 After about 8 minutes, remove the shrimp and also keep warm. Now sear the scallions, add the sprouts and fry all together for 2 minutes.

5 Mix the cornstarch with the stock, stir in the sambal oelek, sugar, lemon juice and tomato paste. Add to the wok, bring to a boil and season with salt.

6 Arrange the noodles in bowls, with the vegetables and shrimp on top, and pour the sauce over.

Tip

Soy bean sprouts are the germinated seeds of soy beans. Do not eat the sprouts raw, they could contain germs. Fresh sprouts should always be rinsed with boiling hot water before eating.

Fried Shrimp
with Noodles and Leeks

*In China, noodles are believed to bring good luck: The longer
they are, the longer the eater's life – so do not break them!*

Ingredients

7 ounces Shanghai noodles

3 tablespoons vegetable oil

9 ounces shrimp (cooked
and peeled)

2 leeks · 3 carrots

1 piece fresh ginger root
(size of a walnut)

$1/2$ cup vegetable stock

1 tablespoon sesame oil

5 tablespoons soy sauce

4 teaspoons sambal oelek

salt · freshly ground pepper

Preparation

SERVES 4

1 Bring plenty of water to a boil in a pan and add the Shanghai
noodles. Remove the pan from the heat and allow the noodles
to swell for about 5 minutes. Stir, pour into a sieve and allow
to drain. Mix the noodles with 1 tablespoon vegetable oil.

2 Rinse the shrimp under cold running water and allow to drain.
Prepare the leek, wash and cut into strips. Peel the carrots
and cut into strips. Peel the ginger and grate finely.

3 Heat the remaining vegetable oil in the wok. Sear the leek and
ginger in the wok for about 2 minutes, stirring constantly,
then remove. Add the carrots to the wok and sear briefly.
Pour in the stock, cover and cook for about 5 minutes until
done. Remove the carrots.

4 Heat the sesame oil in the wok, add the shrimp and fry for
about 2 minutes. Stir in the vegetables and noodles and heat.
Season with soy sauce and sambal oelek, then season to taste
with salt and pepper.

Tip

If using frozen shrimp, allow these to defrost
gently at room temperature. Never defrost shrimp
in the microwave as it makes them tough.

Rice Noodles
with Seafood

*The Chinese like their seafood fresh: The leading roles in this
exquisite noodle fantasy are played by shrimp, squid and mussels*

Ingredients

7 ounces thin rice noodles

4 ounces fresh, unshelled
jumbo shrimp

4 ounces squid (tentacles
removed)

1 large onion

2 each red and green chili
peppers

3 sprigs Thai basil

3 garlic cloves

3 tablespoons vegetable oil

4 ounces clams (shelled)

2 tablespoons oyster sauce

2 tablespoons fish sauce

Preparation

SERVES 4

1 Leave the noodles to swell for 10 minutes in tepid water.
Rinse, strain in a sieve and cut into 2-inch lengths with a pair
of scissors.

2 Rinse, peel and devein the shrimp. Wash and pat dry. Rinse
the squid thoroughly and cut into strips.

3 Peel the onion, wash the chili peppers and seed. Cut the
onion and chili peppers into thin strips. Wash the basil and
shake dry. Pluck the leaves and chop coarsely. Peel and chop
the garlic finely.

4 Heat the oil in the preheated wok. Sear the garlic over medium heat. Add the seafood and stir. Pour in the oyster and
fish sauce.

5 Add the drained rice noodles and fry for about 3 minutes,
stirring constantly. Finally add the basil, chili peppers
and onion. Mix everything together and cook for another
3 minutes.

Tip

The heat of this dish makes it ideal for a light
summer evening meal. If you prefer it milder, use
1 stick finely chopped lemongrass instead of the
chili peppers.

Steamed Cod
with a Duo of Cabbages

Ingredients

2 carrots · 1 leek

6 ounces each Chinese cabbage

and savoy cabbage

4 tablespoons soy bean sprouts

1 ½ pounds cod fillet

2 tablespoons lemon juice

salt · freshly ground pepper

1 tablespoon rice flour

3 shallots

2 stalks lemongrass

2 tablespoons vegetable oil

¾ cup fish stock

1 garlic clove

1 cooked potato

Preparation
SERVES 4

1 Peel the carrots, wash the leek, Chinese cabbage and savoy cabbage well, cut everything
into thin strips. Rinse the bean sprouts in a
sieve with hot water and allow to drain.

2 Rinse the fish, pat dry and cut into bite-size
pieces. Sprinkle with lemon juice, salt, pepper
and toss in rice flour. Peel the shallots and
chop. Cut off the white section of the lemongrass and press flat with a wide knife.

3 Heat the oil in the preheated wok. Sear the
fish, remove and keep warm. Cook the carrots,
leek, Chinese cabbage and savoy cabbage in
the wok until just tender, remove. Sear the
shallots in the oil, add the lemongrass. Pour in
the fish stock. Peel the garlic, chop and add.
Simmer for 3 minutes. Remove the lemongrass
from the sauce.

4 Squeeze the potato through a potato press or
sieve and beat into the sauce with a whisk,
then season with salt and pepper. Add the fish
and the vegetables and heat briefly.

Squid Curls
with Snow Peas

Ingredients

14 ounces small squid

(tentacles removed)

salt · 7 ounces snow peas

14 ounces green bell peppers

2 tablespoons sesame oil

3 chopped garlic cloves

2 teaspoons grated fresh ginger

4 tablespoons light soy sauce

6 tablespoons oyster sauce

4 tablespoons rice wine

½ cup chicken stock

1 ½ tablespoons cornstarch

Preparation

SERVES 4

1 Rinse the squid, pat dry and cut lengthwise into thin strips. Blanch briefly in boiling hot water, pour into a sieve and allow to drain.

2 Prepare and rinse the snow peas. Rinse the bell peppers, seed and cut into thin strips.

3 Heat the wok, add the sesame oil. Stir-fry the garlic and ginger briefly, add the snow peas and bell peppers and fry for another 1-2 minutes. Pour in the soy sauce and oyster sauce, then the rice wine and the stock, allow everything to cook gently for 1 minute. Stir the cornstarch well with a little cold water until smooth, then add to the vegetables and bring to a boil.

4 Add the squid to the vegetables and mix well. Bring to a boil briefly and season to taste. Serve with basmati rice.

Squid Diamonds
on a Bed of Vegetables

*Grand chef cuisine: Serving this quickly prepared classic dish to
company guarantees that your guests will shower you with compliments*

Ingredients

1 ¼ pounds squid (tentacles
removed)

1 ¾ cups snow peas

1 red and 1 yellow bell pepper

1 cucumber (about 7 ounces)

3 garlic cloves

2 red chili peppers

1 bunch Thai basil

3 ½ ounces soy bean sprouts

5 tablespoons peanut oil

3 tablespoons lime juice

4 tablespoons light soy sauce

Preparation

SERVES 4

1 Rinse the squid and pat dry. Cut open the body and score on the inside making a diamond grid pattern. Cut into pieces.

2 Trim and wash the peas. Prepare and wash the bell peppers and cut into thin strips lengthwise. Wash the cucumber, cut in half lengthwise, seed and cut into thin strips. Peel the garlic, wash and seed the chilies and chop finely.

3 Wash the basil, shake dry and pluck off the leaves. Rinse the bean sprouts under hot running water and leave to drain.

4 Heat a wok and add 2 tablespoons of the peanut oil. Stir-fry the squid. Add the chili pepper and garlic and stir-fry for another 5 minutes. Pour in the lime juice and soy sauce and stir well. Remove the squid and keep warm.

5 Heat the remaining oil in the wok. Cook the peas and bell peppers. Add the cucumber and bean sprouts and briefly cook gently. Return the squid and the sauce to the mixture and stir in the basil leaves.

Tip

This dish tastes especially good when made with fresh squid. However, you can use the same quantity of frozen squid rings if fresh squid is not available.

Exotic Stir-fried Rice
with Apples and Fish

*A rice creation with an East-Western touch: Shrimp and fish
meet apples, raisins and bean sprouts for a culinary rendezvous*

Ingredients

1 large onion

3/4 pound fennel

1 red pepper

6 ounces bean sprouts

3 tablespoons sesame oil

1 cup rice

2 tablespoons soy sauce

1 pound ocean perch fillets

1 tablespoon lemon juice

1/2 pound apples

1/4 pound shrimp (cooked
and peeled)

1/2 cup raisins

1 teaspoon dried dill

Preparation

SERVES 4

1 Peel the onion and dice finely. Wash and prepare the fennel
and pepper and cut into thin strips. Rinse the bean sprouts
under hot water and leave to drain.

2 Heat the oil in the preheated wok. Fry the diced onion until
translucent, add the rice and stir-fry briefly. Add the strips
of fennel and pepper and fry all together for about 10 minutes, stirring constantly. Pour in 1 cup water and the soy
sauce and leave to simmer for 25 minutes.

3 Cut the fish into bite-size pieces, sprinkle with lemon juice
and leave to marinate for 10 minutes. Meanwhile peel and
core the apples, quarter and slice thinly.

4 Put the apple slices and fish pieces into the wok and allow
to simmer for 10 minutes. Rinse the shrimp under cold water
in a sieve and allow to drain, then add to the fish rice.

5 Carefully stir in the raisins, bean sprouts and dill. Allow
the flavors to combine for another 2 minutes, then serve
garnished with fresh dill.

Tip

The apples with the best aroma for this stir-fried
rice recipe are a slightly sour variety which will
not soften too quickly when cooked.

Fish Curry
with Spicy Rice

Ingredients

1 ½ cups basmati rice · 3 cloves

1 stick cinnamon · 1 teaspoon

cardamom · 1 ¼ pounds cod fillets

2 shallots · 2 garlic cloves

2 teaspoons freshly grated ginger

root · 2 sprigs cilantro

2 tablespoons sesame oil

4 tablespoons soy sauce

6 tablespoons unsweetened

coconut milk · 2 teaspoons curry

powder · 1 teaspoon chili powder

1 pinch saffron

1 tablespoon ground almonds

1 tablespoon lemon juice

salt · pepper

Preparation

SERVES 4

1 Rinse the rice well under running water and bring to a boil with cloves, cinnamon and cardamom in three cups of water in a pot. Allow to swell for 20 minutes.

2 Rinse the fish, pat dry and cut into bite-size pieces. Peel the shallots and garlic and chop finely. Peel the ginger and grate finely. Wash the cilantro, shake dry, pluck the leaves from the stems and chop coarsely.

3 Heat the oil in the preheated wok. Sear the shallots, then add the garlic and ginger and fry all together.

4 Add the soy sauce and coconut milk. Stir in the curry powder, chili powder, saffron, almonds and lemon juice, season to taste with salt and pepper.

5 Add the fish to the sauce and simmer for about 5 minutes over medium heat, stirring constantly. Finally stir in the chopped cilantro. Serve the fish curry with the spicy rice.

Fish in Rice Paper
with Sesame Seeds

Ingredients

16 sheets rice paper

1 ¼ pounds fish fillet (e.g. cod,
shellfish, perch)

salt · freshly ground pepper

juice of 1 lemon

²/₃ cup vegetable oil

2 tablespoons roasted sesame
seeds

1 garlic clove

2 red chili peppers

1 tablespoon sugar

¹/₃ cup rice vinegar

2 tablespoons each chopped
mint and cilantro leaves

Preparation

SERVES 4

1 Moisten the sheets of rice paper between damp dishtowels. Rinse the fish and pat dry. Cut into 16 pieces, salt and pepper, sprinkle with lemon juice.

2 Place 1 piece of fish on 1 sheet of rice paper. Fold the sides in and roll the sheets up along the long side.

3 Heat the wok, add the oil and fry the rolls in the oil, a few at a time, until golden yellow. Remove, allow to drain on paper towels and sprinkle with sesame seeds.

4 For the sauce, peel the garlic and chop finely. Cut the chili peppers in half lengthwise, seed, wash and chop finely. Mix with sugar, rice vinegar, mint and cilantro. Season to taste with salt and pepper. Serve with the fish parcels.

Fish Bites
with Vegetable Rice

Not the usual fish fingers: Fish bites in a crispy coating
are quick and easy to prepare with a delight in every bite

Ingredients

2 cups basmati rice

1 bunch cilantro

1/2 pound each broccoli and carrots

1/2 cup bean sprouts

1 pound fish fillet (e.g. cod or hake)

6 tablespoons lemon juice

salt

freshly ground pepper

flour, for coating

2 eggs

1 tablespoon sesame oil

1 teaspoon freshly grated ginger root

vegetable oil, for frying

Preparation

SERVES 4

1 Put the rice in a sieve and rinse with cold water, then bring to a boil in 4 cups of water, add salt, cover and leave to simmer for 20 minutes over low heat. Wash the cilantro, shake dry, chop coarsely and mix into the cooked rice.

2 Wash the broccoli and peel the carrots. Separate the broccoli into small flowerets. Cut the carrots into quarters lengthwise, then into small pieces. Rinse the bean sprouts in a sieve under hot running water and allow to drain.

3 Cut the fish into bite-size pieces, sprinkle with lemon juice. Leave to marinate for 5 minutes, then season with salt and pepper. Sprinkle some flour onto a flat plate. Beat the eggs in a deep dish with 1 teaspoon water.

4 Heat the oil in the preheated wok. Stir-fry the vegetables for about 5 minutes. Mix in the bean sprouts and ginger, and season with salt and pepper. Fold the mixed vegetables into the cooked rice.

5 Clean the wok, pour in enough oil for deep-frying and heat. Toss the fish strips in flour, dip in the egg and fry in the hot oil until golden brown. Serve on top of the vegetable rice.

Tip

Serve the fish bites with a tangy apricot dip made from 3 tablespoons soy sauce, 1 teaspoon sambal oelek, 1 tablespoon lemon juice, 4 tablespoons apricot jam and a pinch of ground ginger.

Monkfish Medallions
with Noodles and Mushrooms

While etiquette dictates that mealtimes should be a silent affair,
an exeption is made for noodles which may be eaten with gusto

Ingredients

2 garlic cloves

1 piece fresh ginger root

(size of a walnut)

1 red chili pepper

6 ounces shiitake mushrooms

1 bunch scallions

9 ounces rice noodles · salt

2 tablespoons slivered

almonds

1 1/4 pound monkfish fillet

3 tablespoons vegetable oil

2 tablespoons sesame oil

2 tablespoons soy sauce

4 teaspoons dry sherry

2 tablespoons chopped

cilantro leaves

Preparation

SERVES 4

1 Peel the garlic and ginger and chop finely. Cut the chili pepper in half lengthwise, seed, wash and cut into strips. Prepare the shiitake mushrooms, rub clean with paper towels and slice. Prepare the scallions and cut into $2/3$-inch lengths.

2 Cook the rice noodles in plenty of boiling salted water according to the instructions on the package until just done. Rinse in a sieve under cold running water and allow to drain. Reserve and keep warm.

3 In the preheated wok, roast the almond slivers without oil until golden brown, then remove. Rinse the fish, pat dry and cut into 8 medallions. Heat 2 tablespoons vegetable oil in the preheated wok. Fry the fish medallions for about 1 minute on each side, then remove. Heat the remaining 1 tablespoon oil, add the garlic, ginger, chili, mushrooms and scallions and fry for 2 minutes, stirring constantly.

4 Add the noodles, almonds, sesame oil, soy sauce, sherry and fish and cook briefly. Season to taste and serve garnished with cilantro leaves.

Tip

If monkfish is not available, use any other white fish, but it should be firm so that it doesn't fall apart when cooking. Members of the perch family or cod are particularly suitable.

Sweet and Sour Fish Stew
with Ginger and Bamboo

Ingredients

1 ⅓ pounds mixed fish fillet
(e.g. cod, perch) · 1 piece fresh
ginger root (size of a walnut)

2 garlic cloves · 2 scallions

5 ounces bamboo shoots (canned)

5 ounces button mushrooms

3 tablespoons vegetable oil

4 tablespoons mango chutney

5 tablespoons rice vinegar

4 teaspoons sherry

4 tablespoons soy sauce

2 tablespoons sugar

½ cup vegetable stock

1 level teaspoon cornstarch

salt · freshly ground pepper

Preparation
SERVES 4

1   Rinse the fish, pat dry and cut into bite-size
pieces. Peel the ginger and garlic and chop
finely. Prepare the scallions, wash and cut into
thin strips. Allow the bamboo shoots to drain
in a sieve. Prepare the mushrooms, rub clean
with paper towels and slice finely.

2   Heat the oil in the preheated wok and fry the
fish in the oil. Remove and keep warm.

3   Put the ginger and garlic into the wok and fry
briefly. Add the mushrooms, scallions and
bamboo shoots and stir-fry for about 3 minutes
over medium heat. Stir in the mango chutney,
vinegar, sherry, soy sauce, sugar and stock.

4   Carefully fold in the pieces of fish. Stir the
cornstarch in a small cup with 2 tablespoons
water, then pour over the fish, stir in evenly
and quickly. Allow the fish to simmer for
another 2 minutes, then season to taste with
salt and pepper and serve.

Sea Bass
in Red Sauce

Ingredients

4 ounces hearts of palm (canned)

1 yellow bell pepper

3 scallions

1 piece fresh ginger root

(size of a walnut)

3 garlic cloves

1 pound sea bass fillet

2 $1/2$ teaspoons cornstarch

salt · 3 tablespoons rice wine

6 tablespoons canned tomato

purée (not paste!)

1 tablespoon brown sugar

2 tablespoons rice vinegar

1 tablespoon soy sauce

4 tablespoons peanut oil

Preparation

SERVES 4

1 Allow the hearts of palm to drain in a sieve, and cut into slices. Prepare the bell pepper, wash, seed and cut into thin slices. Prepare the scallions, wash and cut into rings. Peel the ginger and garlic, then chop finely. Cut the fish fillet into strips.

2 Stir 2 tablespoons cornstarch with 1 tablespoon water, a pinch of salt and 1 tablespoon rice wine. Add the fish and allow to marinate for 10 minutes.

3 Stir the tomato purée, sugar, vinegar, 2 tablespoons rice wine and 4 tablespoons water together, then stir in $1/2$ teaspoon cornstarch and the soy sauce.

4 Heat the oil in the preheated wok. Drain the marinated pieces of fish and fry in the oil until golden yellow. Remove and keep warm. Stir-fry the pepper, scallions, ginger and garlic for 4 minutes. Add the hearts of palm and the tomato-soy sauce and simmer for 2 minutes. Add the fish and serve immediately.

Poultry
and Meat

Classic Chicken
Sweet and Sour

*Definitely something special: This ingenious combination of chicken,
aromatic pineapple and spicy hot ginger will give any gourmet wings*

Ingredients

1 piece fresh ginger root (size
of a walnut) · 2 garlic cloves

6 tablespoons light soy sauce

1 tablespoon Chinese five-
spice powder

4 tablespoons rice vinegar

1 1/4 pound skinless, boneless
chicken breast portion

1/4 pineapple

1 bunch scallions · 4 carrots

2 tablespoons vegetable oil

1 2/3 cup chicken stock

3 tablespoons tomato paste

2 teaspoons cornstarch

salt · freshly ground pepper

sugar

Preparation

SERVES 4

1 Peel and chop the ginger and garlic finely. Combine with
the soy sauce, rice vinegar and five-spice powder to make a
marinade. Rinse the chicken, pat dry, cut into bite-size pieces
and leave to marinate, covered with plastic wrap, for about
30 minutes.

2 Peel the pineapple, remove the hard core and cut the flesh
into small pieces. Prepare the scallions, wash and cut diagonally into thin rings. Peel the carrots and cut into thin sticks.

3 Heat the oil in the preheated wok. Drain the chicken, reserving the marinade, and stir-fry in the hot oil until brown on all
sides. Add the scallions and carrots and fry briefly.

4 Mix the reserved marinade with the stock, tomato paste and
cornstarch, add to the chicken and bring to a boil. Stir in
the pineapple, season with salt, pepper and sugar and cook
gently for a few minutes. Serve with basmati rice.

Tip

For variation, try this classic dish with duck breast
(skinless) instead of chicken. Cut the duck into
narrow strips and sear over high heat briefly, so
that it is still pink inside when cut.

Chicken Ragout
with Spring Onions

Practice makes the chef: If you are stir-frying meat that has been marinated, cook it in batches to avoid stewing the meat

Ingredients

1 1/2 cup basmati rice · salt

6 spring onions

6 small carrots

1 1/4 pound skinless, boneless chicken breast portions

freshly ground pepper

4 teaspoons cornstarch

7 ounces soy bean sprouts

4 tablespoons vegetable oil

1 teaspoon ground ginger

4 tablespoons rice wine

4 tablespoons soy sauce

Preparation

SERVES 4

1 Rinse the rice thoroughly in a sieve under running water and cook with 3 cups of water. Add a little salt, cover, reduce the heat and allow to swell over low heat.

2 Prepare the spring onions, wash and cut into rings. Peel the carrots, cut in half lengthwise and then into thin sticks.

3 Rinse the chicken, pat dry and cut crosswise into thin slices. Salt, pepper and dust with cornstarch. Rinse the bean sprouts in a sieve under hot water and allow to drain.

4 Heat the oil in the preheated wok. Stir-fry the chicken until done, remove from the wok and keep warm. Add the spring onions, carrots and bean sprouts to the wok and cook for 5 minutes, stirring occasionally. Season with ginger, rice wine and soy sauce. Bring to a boil, season to taste with salt and a little pepper.

5 Arrange the vegetables on plates with the meat on top. Serve with the basmati rice.

Tip

Ginger has a unique, slightly pungent flavor. Its natural oils stimulate the digestion and strengthen the immune system. Fresh ginger tastes stronger and works better than the powder.

Fried Chicken
with Morel Mushrooms

Ingredients

12 dried morel mushrooms

1 garlic clove

1 green chili pepper

1 1/4 pounds skinless, boneless chicken breast portions

1 tablespoon cornstarch

4 tablespoons soy sauce

1/2 cup rice wine

1 tablespoon grated fresh ginger

1 leek · 5 medium carrots

1 small head cauliflower

2 cups soy bean sprouts · 6 tablespoons soy oil · salt · pepper

1 tablespoon chopped cilantro leaves

Preparation
SERVES 4

1 Leave the morel mushrooms to swell for 30 minutes in tepid water. Peel the garlic, wash and seed the chili pepper. Finely chop the garlic and the chili pepper.

2 Rinse the chicken breast, pat dry and cut into strips. Whisk the cornstarch with the soy sauce and rice wine, then add the ginger, chili and garlic. Add the meat and allow to marinate for 30 minutes. Wash and prepare the vegetables. Cut the leek into rings, the carrots into strips and separate the cauliflower into small flowerets. Rinse the bean sprouts in a sieve under hot running water and allow to drain.

3 Heat 1 tablespoon soy oil in the preheated wok. Drain the chicken, reserving the marinade, and stir-fry the strips in small batches over high heat until brown on all sides. Remove the chicken and keep warm.

4 Heat the remaining oil in the wok and cook the leek, carrots and cauliflower in small batches until tender but firm to the bite. Add the morel mushrooms, bean sprouts and meat. Add the marinade, salt and pepper, simmer briefly and stir in the chopped cilantro leaves.

Chicken and Vegetables
with Glass Noodles

Ingredients

4 skinless, boneless chicken breast
portions · 2 tablespoons soy sauce
1 red, 1 yellow and 1 green
bell pepper · ¼ pound shiitake
mushrooms · ¼ pound snow peas
½ pound Chinese cabbage leaves
1 ½ cups bean sprouts
4 tablespoons sesame oil
1 tablespoon cornstarch · salt
½ tablespoon red curry paste
1 tablespoon grated fresh ginger
root
1 tablespoon chopped cilantro
⅓ pound cooked glass noodles
⅓ cup chicken stock

Preparation
SERVES 4

1 Rinse the chicken breasts, pat dry and cut into
narrow strips. Mix with the soy sauce and
leave to marinate for 30 minutes. Preheat the
oven to 450°F.

2 Cut the peppers in half lengthwise, seed and
remove the membranes. Wash the halves and
roast in the oven, skin side up, until the skin
turns brown and blisters. Allow to cool under
a clean dishtowel, pull off the skin and cut the
peppers into thin strips.

3 Prepare the shiitake mushrooms, rub clean with
paper towels and slice thinly. Rinse the snow
peas and Chinese cabbage leaves. Shred the
Chinese cabbage leaves coarsely. Rinse the bean
sprouts in a sieve under hot running water and
allow to drain.

4 Heat 3 tablespoons oil in the wok and sear the
vegetables. Add salt, remove and keep warm.
Dust the chicken with cornstarch and sear in
the remaining oil. Stir in the curry paste, ginger and cilantro. Add the noodles and vegetables, pour in the stock. Allow all to simmer for
another 2 minutes.

Chicken Fritters
with Sesame Seeds

*Lovely and crunchy: While deep-frying is not something you
do every day, it is a great way to prepare food for a party*

Ingredients

1 egg white

1 cup all-purpose flour

3 tablespoons cornstarch

2 teaspoons baking powder

salt · freshly ground pepper

½ cup vegetable oil

1 tablespoon grated fresh
ginger root

7 tablespoons soy sauce

5 tablespoons rice wine

1 ¼ pounds skinless, boneless
chicken breast portions

4 medium carrots

2 bunches scallions

½ pound bean sprouts

2 tablespoons sesame seeds

vegetable oil, for deep-frying

Preparation
SERVES 4

1 To make the batter, whisk the egg white until stiff. Mix together the flour, cornstarch, baking powder, salt and pepper in a small bowl. Fold the flour mixture and the water into the egg white, a spoonful at a time. Finally stir in 6 tablespoons of the oil. Leave the batter to stand for 30 minutes.

2 Mix the ginger with 2 tablespoons each of the soy sauce and the rice wine. Drizzle the marinade over the meat, cover and set side.

3 Peel the carrots and cut into strips. Trim and wash the scallions and cut on the slant into 1-inch lengths. Rinse the bean sprouts in a sieve under hot running water and leave to drain.

4 Heat 2 tablespoons of the remaining oil in the preheated wok. Stir-fry the carrots and scallions. Pour in the rest of the soy sauce, rice wine and 3 tablespoons water and allow to simmer for 5 minutes. Stir in the bean sprouts, heat briefly and season to taste. Set the vegetables aside and keep warm.

5 Clean the wok and heat the oil for deep-frying. Fold the sesame seeds into the batter. Dip the pieces of chicken into the batter and fry in batches in the hot oil for about 3 minutes each. Remove and drain on paper towels. Serve with the vegetables.

Tip

This batter is also suitable for other white meats, such as turkey or veal. You can also make delicious fritters in this way with pieces of fish or blanched vegetables.

Chicken Curry
Indian Style

Ingredients

4 small skinless, boneless chicken breast portions

grated rind of ½ lemon

1 tablespoon lemon juice

1 teaspoon sambal oelek

1 teaspoon sugar

salt · freshly ground pepper

½ teaspoon ground coriander

3 scallions · 11 ounces green beans · 2 garlic cloves · 4 tablespoons sesame oil · 1 teaspoon freshly grated ginger root

1 teaspoon ground turmeric

1 tablespoon curry powder

1 ½ cups unsweetened coconut milk

Preparation
SERVES 4

1 Rinse the chicken breasts, pat dry and cut into strips. Stir the lemon peel and juice, sambal oelek, sugar, salt, pepper and coriander together. Add the chicken and allow to marinate for about 20 minutes.

2 Rinse the scallions, cut the white section into quarters lengthwise, then cut everything into 1-inch pieces. Trim and rinse the beans, cut in half and cook for 10 minutes in salted water until done. Pour into a sieve, rinse with cold water and allow to drain.

3 Drain the chicken, reserving the marinade. Peel the garlic and chop finely. Heat the oil in the preheated wok and sear the meat. Add the onions and garlic, and stir-fry briefly. Add the ginger, turmeric, curry powder, the reserved marinade and the coconut milk and allow all to simmer for 5 minutes.

4 Add the beans to the wok and season the chicken curry to taste. Garnish with cilantro leaves (optional) before serving.

Turkey Curry
with Coconut Milk

Ingredients

1 ¼ pounds turkey breast portions

1 red bell pepper

½ pound scallions

1 large bunch fresh basil

1 ⅔ cups unsweetened coconut milk

1 tablespoon yellow curry paste

2 tablespoons soy sauce

1 tablespoon sugar

Preparation

SERVES 4

1 Rinse the turkey breast and pat dry. With a sharp kitchen knife, cut first into ½-inch slices, then into fine strips.

2 Cut the red bell pepper into half lengthwise, seed, wash and cut into fine strips. Trim and wash the scallions and cut into ½-inch rings. Wash the basil and shake dry. Pluck the leaves from the stems. Finely chop half the leaves and reserve the rest for garnishing.

3 Bring the coconut milk to a boil in a wok, stir in the curry paste and simmer for 1 minute. Add the turkey breast and simmer for another 4 minutes, stirring occasionally.

4 Add the prepared vegetables and simmer everything for another 3 minutes. Stir in the chopped basil, soy sauce and sugar and season to taste. Serve the curry with the reserved basil leaves.

Breast of Duck
with Cilantro Noodles

*Fancy something exotic? Tender duck breast, honey and spicy
cilantro provide a real culinary delight for everyone*

Ingredients

3/4 pound Chinese egg noodles

(e.g. Hokkien)

salt

1 1/3 pounds duck breast

1 tablespoon honey

4 tablespoons soy sauce

1/2 teaspoon sambal oelek

1 red bell pepper

1 bunch scallions

3 tablespoons vegetable oil

2 tablespoons lemon juice

1 cup chicken stock

2 tablespoons chopped

cilantro

Preparation

SERVES 4

1 Cook the noodles in a generous amount of boiling salted water according to the instructions on the package, strain in a sieve, rinse under cold water and allow to drain.

2 Cut the duck breast into thin slices. Stir the honey together with the soy sauce and sambal oelek. Add the meat and leave to marinate for 30 minutes.

3 Wash, halve and seed the red pepper. Rinse the halves, then cut into fine strips. Trim and wash the scallions. Cut the green part into rings, and the white part into fine strips.

4 Remove the meat from the marinade, drain and reserve the marinade. Heat 1 tablespoon oil in the preheated wok. Stir-fry the duck breast slices over high heat until brown, then remove. Fry the red bell pepper and the scallions in the wok in the remaining oil until just tender. Season with salt and lemon juice. Pour in the stock and reserved marinade. Add the duck breast and noodles, bring to a boil, sprinkle with cilantro and serve.

Tip

You can also use boneless turkey or chicken breast instead of the duck breast. If using turkey or chicken, spice up the marinade with an additional 2 tablespoons lime juice and 1 teaspoon honey.

Fried Rice
with Duck Breast

Ingredients

2 duck breast fillets (about

$1/2$ pound each)

salt · freshly ground pepper

2 tablespoons oil

1 leek

2 carrots

$1/2$ pineapple

1 red chili pepper

1 tablespoon freshly grated

ginger root

1 pound cooked long-grain rice

2 tablespoons soy sauce

2 tablespoons dry sherry

5 tablespoons chicken stock

Preparation

SERVES 4

1 Preheat the oven to 350°F. Salt and pepper the duck breasts. Heat the oil in the preheated wok and sear the duck breasts, skin side down, over high heat for 3-4 minutes. Turn and fry for another 4-5 minutes. Remove the duck breasts from the wok and bake in the preheated oven for about 10 minutes, with the skin side up, until done.

2 Prepare the leek, wash and cut into fine rings. Peel the carrots and pineapple. Cut the carrots into thin strips, the pineapple into small pieces.

Cut the chili pepper in half lengthwise, seed, wash and cut into strips.

3 Fry the leek, carrots and pineapple in the oil left from frying the duck breasts. Stir in the chili pepper, ginger and rice. Season to taste with soy sauce, sherry and stock. Cut the duck breasts (they should be pink inside) into thin slices and mix into the rice.

Breast of Duck
on Green Noodles

Ingredients

¹/₂ pound Japanese green noodles

1 tablespoon honey

4 tablespoons soy sauce

¹/₂ teaspoon sambal oelek

2 boneless duck breasts (about
1 ¹/₄ pounds)

3 tablespoons oil

salt

2 tablespoons lemon juice

4 tablespoons chicken stock

1 scallion

Preparation

SERVES 4

1   Cook the noodles in salted, boiling water according to the instructions on the package, pour into a sieve, rinse with cold water and allow to drain.

2   Mix the honey, soy sauce and sambal oelek together in a small bowl for the marinade. Cut the duck breasts into strips, add to the bowl, cover and leave to marinate for 30 minutes. Drain the duck, reserving the marinade.

3   Heat the oil in the preheated wok and sear the duck briefly. Season with salt and lemon juice, remove and keep warm. Pour the stock and the reserved marinade into the wok, add the noodles and heat.

4   Trim the scallion, wash and cut into rings. Shape the noodles into nests and arrange the duck breasts on top. Sprinkle with scallion rings and garnish with fresh herbs (optional).

Sweet and Sour Pork
with Pineapple and Tomatoes

Not only a big favorite in China: The abundance of simple ingredients makes this classic specialty simply irresistible

Ingredients

1 ½ pounds pork tenderloin

1 piece fresh ginger root

(size of a walnut)

4 garlic cloves

3 red chili peppers

½ pound tomatoes

1 pound fresh pineapple

2 tablespoons sesame oil

2 tablespoons sunflower oil

4 tablespoons rice vinegar

4 tablespoons light soy sauce

4 teaspoons sherry

2 tablespoons sugar

1 cup chicken stock

2 level teaspoons cornstarch

Preparation

SERVES 4

1 Cut the pork with a sharp kitchen knife, first crosswise into slices, then the slices into strips. Peel the ginger and slice very thinly. Peel the garlic and chop finely. Prepare, seed, halve and wash the chili peppers, then cut into very fine strips.

2 Cut an X into the top and bottom of the tomatoes. Put into boiling hot water for a few seconds. The skin should come off now. Peel, halve, seed and dice the tomatoes. Peel the pineapple, remove the core and cut the flesh into chunks.

3 Heat the sesame oil and sunflower oil in the preheated wok. Stir-fry the meat. Add the ginger, garlic and chilies and briefly stir-fry together. Add the tomatoes and pineapple and stir-fry for another 1-2 minutes. Add the vinegar, soy sauce, sherry and sugar. Pour in ¾ cup of the stock and mix well.

4 Stir the cornstarch into the remaining stock and pour evenly over the meat. Mix everything thoroughly and leave to simmer for about 3 minutes.

Tip

This dish belongs to the great classics of Chinese cuisine. It tastes just as good with chicken breast or turkey breast instead of pork. To save time, you may want to use canned pineapple chunks.

Stir-fry
with Pork Tenderloin

Little effort, but great effect: This stir-fry is ready in
no time and tastes so good that you will not get enough of it

Ingredients

14 ounces pork tenderloin

3 tablespoons oyster sauce

1/2 teaspoon freshly ground
pepper

2 1/4 cups drained canned
bamboo shoots

4 ounces leaf spinach

5 tablespoons sesame oil

1 tablespoon yellow curry
paste

2 teaspoons sugar

2 tablespoons lime juice

1 lime

Preparation

SERVES 4

1 Cut the meat into bite-size pieces, mix with the oyster sauce and pepper and allow to marinate for about 15 minutes.

2 Drain the bamboo shoots and cut into fine strips. Prepare the spinach, wash and allow to drain. Remove any tough stalks.

3 Heat the oil in the preheated wok. Stir-fry the meat for about 2 minutes over high heat. Add the curry paste and mix well, then add the bamboo strips and the spinach. Season with sugar and lime juice and cook for another 2 minutes over high heat, stirring constantly.

4 Wash the lime, rub dry and cut into wedges. Arrange the stir-fry in bowls, garnish with the lime wedges and serve. Basmati rice goes very well with this dish.

Tip

Of course, this stir-fry can also be prepared with other meats, beef for example. In this case, make it a little hotter by adding, for example, 3 tablespoons red curry paste.

Tenderloin of Pork
with Lime and Garlic

How convenient: The addition of lime juice to a marinade is not just for flavor but also to tenderize the meat

Ingredients

1 red bell pepper

4 garlic cloves

6 tablespoons soy sauce

4 teaspoons lime juice

8 tablespoons fish sauce

1 teaspoon freshly ground white pepper

2/3 cup beef or chicken stock

1 teaspoon cornstarch

1 1/4 pounds tenderloin of pork

2 tablespoons vegetable oil

7 ounces Japanese udon noodles

salt · 1/2 bunch scallions

Preparation

SERVES 4

1 Prepare the pepper, wash and dice finely. Peel the garlic and chop finely. Mix both with the soy sauce, lime juice, fish sauce, pepper, stock and cornstarch. Add the meat and leave to marinate for 30 minutes.

2 Preheat the oven to 350°F. Remove the meat from the marinade and allow to drain, reserving the marinade. Heat the oil in the preheated wok. Stir-fry the meat in the hot oil. Place in the oven and roast for about another 15 minutes until done, adding the marinade 5 minutes before the end of the roasting time.

3 Cook the udon noodles in plenty of boiling salted water until just tender according to the instructions on the package. Pour into a sieve and allow to drain. Prepare the scallions, wash and cut the green diagonally into rings.

4 To serve, mix the noodles with the sauce and cut the meat into slices. Arrange in small bowls and garnish with the scallion green.

Tip

Udon noodles are made from wheat flour. They are a favorite of Japanese cuisine. As an alternative, you could use Chinese egg noodles or any other narrow egg noodles if no Asian food store is near.

Pork Tenderloin
with Savoy Cabbage

Ingredients

1 ¼ pounds savoy cabbage

½ pound shiitake mushrooms

1 small onion

2 garlic cloves

1 ¼ pounds pork tenderloin

salt · freshly ground pepper

3 tablespoons vegetable oil

1 teaspoon grated fresh ginger root

1 tablespoon curry powder

6 tablespoons beef or chicken stock

3 tablespoons soy sauce

1 tablespoon chopped fresh parsley

Preparation

SERVES 4

1 Halve the cabbage, remove the outer leaves and core. Finely shred the halves, rinse and allow to drain in a sieve. Rub the mushrooms clean with paper towels and slice thinly. Peel the onion and the garlic and chop finely.

2 With a sharp kitchen knife, cut the meat across the grain first into slices and then into strips. Season with salt and pepper.

3 Heat the oil in the preheated wok and stir-fry the meat over high heat. Remove the meat from the wok and keep warm.

4 Reduce the heat and stir-fry the cabbage, adding in gradually the onions, garlic and mushrooms. Season with ginger, curry powder and pepper, then pour in the stock and soy sauce. Briefly bring to a boil. Before serving, stir in the meat and parsley.

Stir-fried Beef
with Vegetables and Sherry

Ingredients

1 pound carrots

1/2 pound leek

1 stalk celery

1 red bell pepper

1/2 pound rump roast

3 tablespoons vegetable oil

1/2 cup dry sherry

2/3 cup frozen peas

2 tablespoons soy sauce

salt · freshly ground pepper

1 tablespoon curry powder

1 teaspoon hoisin sauce

2 tablespoons fresh parsley
leaves

Preparation

SERVES 4

1 Prepare and wash the vegetables. Slice the carrots, leeks and celery sticks finely. Cut the bell pepper into fine strips.

2 With a sharp kitchen knife, cut the rump steak across the grain into narrow strips.

3 Heat the oil in the preheated wok. Stir-fry the strips of meat for about 5 minutes over high heat. Remove the meat and keep warm.

4 Reduce the heat and gradually stir-fry all the vegetables in batches. Add the sherry, stir in the peas and season with the soy sauce, salt, pepper, curry powder and hoisin sauce.

5 Cook the vegetables for about 2 more minutes, then season generously with salt and pepper. Finally stir in the beef and parsley leaves. Serve the stir-fried beef with basmati rice or any other Asian rice.

Stir-fried Beef
with Orange Wedges

Here the predominating flavor is sweetness: Honey and orange add new fascinating overtones to this classic beef dish

Ingredients

3/4 cup basmati rice

salt · 1 orange

2 scallions

3/4 pound beef (for stir-frying, e.g. sirloin steak)

freshly ground pepper

2 tablespoons sesame oil

2/3 cup orange juice

1 tablespoon light soy sauce

1 tablespoon honey

Preparation

SERVES 4

1 Rinse the rice in a sieve until the water runs clear. Bring to a boil in a pan with 1 1/2 cups of water. Salt, cover, reduce the heat and allow to swell for about 20 minutes over low heat.

2 Wash the orange and rub dry. With a zester, pull off fine zests from the peel. Peel the orange, removing also the white pith, and separate into wedges. Lift the fruit segments out from their membranes, catching any juice. Prepare the scallions, wash and cut into rings. Cut the meat across the grain into strips, salt and pepper. Heat the oil in the preheated wok. Stir-fry the meat over high heat for 3 minutes, then remove from the wok and keep warm.

3 Add the white of the scallions to the remaining oil in the wok and stir-fry. Add the orange juice, soy sauce and honey and cook until syrupy. Season with salt and pepper. Add the orange wedges and the meat, heat and stir in the green of the scallions. Arrange the beef on the rice and garnish with orange zests.

Tip

If you don't have a zester, you could also peel the rind thinly with a very sharp knife and cut it into fine strips.

Thai Salad
with Stir-fried Beef

Let's get really exotic: Most Thai salads are a delicate combination of apparently opposing textures and flavors

Ingredients

1 ½ pounds beef (cut for
roast beef)

1 tablespoon clarified butter

about ¾ pound mixed salad
greens and vegetables
(e.g. spinach, bean sprouts,
bell peppers, Thai basil)

2 red chili peppers

1 garlic clove

6 tablespoons lemon juice

6 tablespoons olive oil

1 teaspoon sesame oil

1 teaspoon soy sauce

1 teaspoon fish sauce

1 teaspoon sugar

1 teaspoon freshly grated
ginger root

salt · freshly ground pepper

4 ounces cashew nuts

Preparation

SERVES 4

1 Remove any sinews and skin from the beef if necessary. Heat the clarified butter in the preheated wok and stir-fry the beef for about 20 minutes, turning frequently. Reserve, wrap in aluminium foil and allow to rest for 5 minutes.

2 Prepare the ingredients for the salad, wash or rinse, allow to drain and cut or pluck into bite-size pieces.

3 For the dressing, cut the chili peppers in half lengthwise, seed and wash. Peel the garlic and chop both finely. Mix the chili peppers and garlic with the lemon juice, olive oil, sesame oil, soy sauce, fish sauce, sugar and ginger. Season the dressing to taste with salt and pepper. Mix half the dressing with the salad ingredients and toss lightly.

4 Slice the roast beef thinly across the grain. Arrange the salad on a large dish or plate and top with the beef slices. Drizzle with the remaining dressing.

5 Roast the cashew nuts in a pan without oil until golden yellow. Chop coarsely and sprinkle over the salad.

Tip

Rare beef salad is a traditional dish from northeastern Thailand. The dressing can be seasoned with ground chili pepper for all those who like it extra hot.

Grilled Beef
with Spring Onions

*This is something for everyone's palate: Marinated slices
of beef, grilled and served with spring onions on thin rice noodles*

Ingredients

1 1/4 pounds beef tenderloin

4 tablespoons vegetable oil

2 tablespoons soy sauce

1/2 teaspoon ground pepper

1/2 bunch spring onions

1 garlic clove

1/2 pound thin rice noodles

salt

1 teaspoon freshly grated

ginger root

4 tablespoons oyster sauce

4 tablespoons rice wine

2 tablespoons chopped,

unsalted peanuts

Preparation

SERVES 4

1 Cut the meat across the grain into bite-size slices. For the marinade, mix 2 tablespoons oil, soy sauce and pepper, add the slices of meat, cover and allow to marinate for about 30 minutes.

2 Prepare the scallions and wash, quarter the white lengthwise and cut into pieces about 1 1/2-inches long. Peel the garlic and chop finely. Switch on the grill.

3 Remove the meat from the marinade, allow to drain and place on the oiled grate. Slide under the hot grill and grill on both sides.

4 Cook the rice noodles in boiling salted water according to the instructions on the package, rinse with cold water and allow to drain in a sieve.

5 Heat the remaining oil in the wok. Sear the scallions, ginger and garlic in the oil briefly. Add the oyster sauce and rice wine and cook for about 2 minutes over medium heat.

6 Divide the noodles among small bowls, arrange the meat with the scallions on top and sprinkle with the peanuts. Garnish with cilantro leaves (optional).

Tip

If you have enough time, leave the meat to marinate a little longer. That way, it will take on more aroma and become more tender. Reserve the marinade when draining the meat and use it for the sauce.

Index of recipes

Copyright

Photo Credits

Cover photos: Susie Eising (front cover);
Walter Cimbal (back cover center and bottom);
Jo Kirchherr (back cover top)
Walter Cimbal: 2–3, 9 center and bottom, 25,
29, 61, 67, 70–71, 87, 98–99, 115; Jo Kirch-
herr: 8, 9 top, 10–11, 13, 15, 16, 19, 20, 23,
31, 33, 35, 37, 38, 39, 41, 45, 47, 49, 53,
59, 62, 63, 69; StockFood/Chris Alack: 79,
90; StockFood/Klaus Arras: 21; StockFood/
Bayside: 108, 117; StockFood/Uwe Bender:
81, 109; StockFood/Harry Bischof: 95; Stock-
Food/Michael Boyny: 85; StockFood/Michael
Brauner: 7 (2nd from top left); StockFood/
Jean Cazals: 91, 113, 125; StockFood/James
Duncan: 73, 111; StockFood/S. & P. Eising:

6 left, 42–43, 56, 57, 68, 75, 76, 83, 89, 93,
96, 97, 101; StockFood/Susie Eising: 1, 4–5,
26, 27, 50, 51, 65, 77, 104, 105, 112, 120,
121; StockFood/Luzia Ellert: 7 bottom left;
StockFood/Gabula Art-Foto: 7 center; Stock-
Food/Ulrike Köb: 17; StockFood/David Loftus:
127; StockFood/Joris Luyten: 123; Stock-
Food/Kai Mewes: 103; StockFood/Minh &
Wass: 7 (2nd from bottom left); StockFood/
Snowflake Studios Inc. 55; StockFood/Maximi-
lian Stock LTD: 6 right, 7 top left, 7 right;
StockFood/Jan-Peter Westermann: 84, 107;
StockFood/Frank Wieder: 119